THE ART OF
EASING CONFLICT

by

Miriam Logan

ORIGINAL WRITING

ISBN: 978-1-906018-76-4

A CIP catalogue for this book is available from
the National Library.

Published by Original Writing Ltd., Dublin, 2008.

Printed by Cahills, Dublin.

ACKNOWLEDGEMENTS

Like all creative projects, writing THE ART OF EASING CONFLICT has taken time, concentration and the support of many different people to see it over the finish line. Although it would be impossible to name everyone, I do need to mention some important strands of support that are woven into this book. Let me begin with those who engaged in the development of the Family Mediation Service in Ireland. To the teachers, colleagues and the many people I was privileged to work with in the first ten years of the setting up of that service. In the rich mix of experience within that group, time, energy and scholarship were given to building the skills and practice wisdoms that have influenced me when writing this book. I say thank you to the pioneering team, Maura Wall Murphy, Delma Sweeney, Mary Lloyd, Anna Connelly and Geoffrey Corry. I want to thank in particular Delma Sweeney and Mary Lloyd who inspired me by their dedicated willingness to put patience, energy and creativity into the often challenging dimensions of working at the interface where Psychosocial Dynamics, Economics, and Law come together in the practice of Mediation.

For the lessons in trusting the experiential of the creative, thanks is due to Boann Artists Group who walked the talk, sharing the process of exploration, cross-fertilization and expression of individual creativity with all its gifts and challenges. Thanks to all the members of the group for the stimulation, team spirit, and creativity, in particular Nanette Ledwith, Aine Dunn, Susan Connolly, Anne Marie Moroney and Mary McDonald.

Thank you is due to another strand of support that has been available to me over the years of writing this book. The Religious Society of Friends has a Peace Testimony that continues to inspire me and to have relevance. Having the company of those who search for everyday approaches to peacemaking and the opportunity to attend the silent meditative meetings of Friends has been of great benefit.

Special thanks to all those who have been so constant in their support over the time I have been writing. Everything from conversations over cups of coffee and fun to discussion, critique and book referencing have kept this project alive during the everyday goings and comings of combining family and work life. In particular to Andrew and Leonie Workman, Eileen Mc Glew, Judith Leech, Jill Trapnell, Cora Pollard, Patricia Dunn, Jean Connolly, Eilish Craig, Denise Walsh, Therese O Dowd, Brideen Cannon, Claire Counihan, who have all at differing times encouraged perseverence.

Thank you especially to Mary O'Shea for reading and giving helpful feedback. Thanks also to Original Writing for getting this book to print. Thanks to artist, John ffrench for his kind permission to use a detail from his batik work on the front cover.

To Garrett Burns for getting the process started. To Dorethee Krien, for her help with proofreading. To those I have not named I say thanks also. However lastly and so importantly; thanks to my family, my husband Michael and Sam, our son, to my mother Nancy, my sisters and brothers and for my wider extended family without whose combined spirit this book would not have been possible.

CONTENTS

INTRODUCTION
THE ART OF EASING CONFLICT

An old wisdom

The art of the mediator is a back-to-basics approach that aims to bring ease to conflicts.

It is an unchanging philosophy, with roots traceable back thousands of years to the teachings of the Tao in ancient China. Writings from that time tell us, conflict is a prison that becomes more dangerous the longer we are in it. Yet conflict is part and parcel of our human landscape. It arises easily and naturally in the course of living in a complex world. From a mediator's viewpoint, conflict is neither bad nor difficult; only the troublesome, agitated and resistant behaviours that flow from power struggles are seen as problematic. In taking a view of conflict, the metaphor of the iceberg is sometimes used - most of it lies beneath the surface. Not surprisingly, getting to these underlying issues really matters.

Divisive conflict is commonplace, so much so that people worldwide continue to search for answers to the question - why we humans trap ourselves in conflict and

miss out on life. In *Bridging Cultural Conflicts*, Michelle
LeBaron says:

"Conflict, put simply, is a difference that matters. It
may happen between two people, or between or among
groups over any number of different ideas, needs, goals
or approaches. Some conflicts may easily be solved by
correcting miscommunication or finding a way to satisfy
everyone. But many conflicts go deeper than this, elicit-
ing strong emotions and sensations." From experience, I
know that, beyond the tensions they produce, it is actually our differences that make us creative. They are the
progenitors of change and growth. It is our combined
differences that help us cross-fertilize, complement and
innovate.

When we are in harmony with the creative we accept that differences are central to living. Harmony has
been described rather well by Michelangelo, who saw it
as "the simultaneous existence of differences."

Over the years I have gained great respect for the fact
that seemingly small tensions can escalate and destroy
peace, not just in families but in the workplace, within
communities and between countries. Because interpersonal conflict can put us off-balance, we cannot overplay
the importance of resolving it.

A living, creative art

Easing conflict is a living creative art that takes hold
at a personal level. We might say that the art of easing

conflict is actually the art of unleashing our natural creativity.

Creativity asks that we stop any tendency to get bogged down in absolute stands on what is right and wrong. It moves us off fixed positions and makes possible the conditions for problem solving. The Sufi poet Rumi nicely captures the spirit in the lines: "Out beyond ideas of wrong doing and right doing there is a field; I will meet you there." In this frame of mind we make time and space to move beyond problems to collaboration and resolve - beyond conflicts to creativity. The art of easing conflict is the mediator's stock in trade, drawing on time-honoured principles that work step-by-step to unleash creativity in the parties that are experiencing conflict. The mediator believes that creativity is innate and works to generate the conditions that get it flowing. 'Out of conflict into creativity' might well be the stated hope of a would-be mediator. Empowering that course is always a central aim.

The steps used by the mediator to ease conflict may seem trivial to the uninitiated. But there is a sustainable wisdom inherent in the process that can be of benefit to each of us in our daily lives. For now, let me cut to the chase and say that, if one word could capture the ideas, tone and spirit of how the mediator eases conflict, the word *creativity* might do it.

Most people think of creativity as a quality available only to artists, yet psychologist Jerome Bruner suggests that the condition of creativity arises universally: "Creativity may express itself in one's dealing with children, in making love, in carrying on a business, in formulating physical theory, in painting a picture."

Creativity has the effect of surprise, putting things in new ways which ask us to look with fresh eyes - to stop, to reinterpret, to change, to renew. Each of us is imbued with a creative nature, yet we must empower it.

Creatively-empowered people can change landscapes and build communities. In fact, people are the channels through which creative change can happen. As the world throws up challenges - greater and more complex than before - having a handle on what releases creativity has never been more relevant. A long shadow of toxic fight lies behind us; it is a shadow that dulls trust and encodes the habit of fear. But fighting, and a belief in the usefulness of it, is a paradigm that needs to change. Destroying is not a sign of power; the creative imperative is real power. The power to be creative can change our future.

To promote hopefulness, we must keep a discerning focus on the small, sequential steps that nourish our creativity. When we do our part it has a ripple effect that gives impetus to world harmony.

Creative empowerment

Today's zeitgeist asks for more creative fluency. Creativity is needed in every aspect of living. The fallacy that someone else will make things better has run its course. Although most of my work experience centres on easing family conflict, I know that creative empowerment can be used anywhere. Today we need to take responsibility for this innate gift so that we can work with a variety of world challenges; we need to access our creativity in order to harmonize diversity and get along with each other. To make communities safer and families happier we need our creativity. Again, it will take creative gestures to make the changes needed to stem ecological destructiveness, to heal institutions and business corporations. Indeed, we must master the art of staying creative with conflict in much the same way as all arts are mastered. Psychologist Erich Fromm believes that mastering an art has certain requirements. He tells us we need commitment. We need to bring discipline to the task on hand. Alongside this we need concentration, patience and regular practice. A tall order and one he rightly suggests would fit more easily in our grandfather's time when life was less rushed. If you observe people with a creative spirit they often make it appear effortless - a matter of luck. Artfulness is like that; it often belies the fact that certain basics must exist to bring it about.

Creativity and conflict - can we choose?

Conflict and creativity are sometimes said to be two sides of the same coin - this pairing suggests that, so close are they to each other, a toss one way can mean *conflict* has the upper hand; flip again and *creativity* wins the day. Not so. By gift of being human we can consciously choose our attitudes. Daily we are challenged to decide. The choices we make can influence whether we stay creative or land in conflict; equipping ourselves with what it takes to choose wisely is vital. Unfurling our innate creativity is not a matter of chance; indeed, creativity is nurtured and grounded in the ordinariness of everyday experiences. As we become aware that we have a choice about whether we act to promote conflict or creativity, we can remain committed to learning what it takes to stay creative.

Conflict and creativity are common modes for most of us. At times we all have experiences where we stay creative, generating trust and upbeat loving emotions, and others where we tip into conflict, leading us into negative spirals that eclipse feelings of trust. Mostly, however, we are not bothered enough to analyse how or why this happens. Both conflict and creativity have their own *modi operandi*. In conflict we fuel fear while in creativity we build trust.

Creativity operates through co-operation, collaboration and innovation. Conflict, on the other hand, moves us reactively to avoidance or force. Destructive conflict is bred from force and disrespect for ourselves and others. Cycles of conflict can be driven by fear and these in turn provoke ongoing spirals of high arousal that sabotage problem-solving and put us into patterns of want, wastage and stagnation. On the other hand, as creativity is empowered we build a trust in its power to find paths, open doors and solve problems. In this we learn that survival in a civilized world favours co-operation, harmony and, ultimately, true creativity.

By its nature, conflict leads us towards win-lose, to opposition where 'either/or' thinking dominates. In climates of conflict we are taken into power struggles that breed cycles of powerlessness and fear. Creativity, by its nature, encourages us towards 'yes/and,' to win-win. Creativity empowers us and, because it does, in climates where a creative attitude takes hold we begin to value connections between ourselves and others, to sidestep fear so that trust can flow. Self and other are seen as part of the creative web of life and in this frame we make a giant leap towards the inclusive spirit that rests at the heart of well-being. Working as a mediator, being mindful of both conflict and creativity, is my job and now, after years of working in the field, I am struck by how quickly people release their creativity when the deeper humanitarian issues common to all of us are addressed. Each of us when we are party to a conflict has a fear of being on the losing side. Win-win is the term that captures the essence of collaboration; it also speaks to the central aim of the mediator who, as an impartial third party, aims to bring harmony to troubling issues. Using the principle of win-win, the mediator knows that peace blooms quickest when we stay with the possibility of a good outcome for everyone involved. Balancing all their interests is the guiding principle.

To ease conflict we must learn that harmony in living organic systems is not brought about by force. As crazy and contradictory as it seems, we often think we can force solutions in our conflicts. In practice I have found this viewpoint unworkable. Usually people show up at mediation because they have lost hope in forced solutions and want to go back to first principles of what it means to live fairly. When we are stuck in a conflict, we may believe there is no other way. When we are using opposition, force and attack we may see a fight to the bitter end as our only way through. Science tells us that subtle balancing processes are always at play in our life systems. Einstein said that life is "subtle but not malicious." All living systems seek equilibrium. Action in one direction will seek equal and opposite action. Balancing our differing interests when, as happens in life, we encounter feelings, behaviours and situations that try, annoy and provoke us - while a basic requirement - can require careful handling. Yes, we all meet conflicts that challenge and, indeed, it is commonplace for us to avoid or become aggravated when we are faced with frustrations that seem to threaten us in some way. When we are conscious of these responses we can learn what their function is - what they are telling us we need to learn about the situation in which we find ourselves. They can alert us to the changes we need to make to balance things. The following is an everyday occurrence from life that will illustrate what I mean.

Everyday conflict

Z and B were a couple who found themselves trapped in a toxic conflict. Their relationship had all the characteristics of a destructive power struggle that had become harrowing for everyone involved.

Z and B came to mediation in a deeply upset state, each reporting that their marriage had deteriorated over a number of years and they now viewed it as abusive and disrespectful. Each perceived the other as being at fault and the blame game had been going on for years. Over time, it emerged that their behaviours had become increasingly uncooperative, leading to alternating patterns of fighting and not talking.

They both had a catalogue detailing the 'wrongdoing of the other.' Yet, worryingly, they never managed to clear the air after their quarrels. Little by little, hope for their marriage was breaking down. It was easy to empathise with how distressing life became as these behaviours played out on the surfaces of the couple's lives. They had both lost hope in their ability to be creative. By now they were unwilling to work on meeting their mutual needs and each had become intolerant of their differences. Both agreed that the ongoing conflict was harrowing and debilitating. It left them with a range of anxious feelings. Without cooperation little was working well, either practically or emotionally. Both felt short-changed, lonely and undervalued. Their rows had more than once frightened their on-looking children. In fact, they agreed this was the factor that had led them to pick up the phone and call a mediator.

Inarguably, for Z and B, this was a very sorry state of affairs - yet such situations are also a common symptom of everyday interpersonal conflict when stress levels rise and little insight exists about the real source of the problems.

Getting the Love You Want by Harville Hendrix is a guide for couples who want to make changes in their relationships. He wrote that he had worked with people who had named their fights the 'Three o' Clockers' - because these sessions lasted until three in the morning. Such fights left both feeling depressed for days and resolved nothing. Hendrix, a psychologist, added that, after recounting four or five versions of what was essentially the same argument, the couple were able to see what their fights had in common: "At first, they found it amusing to reduce their fights to the lowest common denominators ... but then a sadness crept into the discussion ... they wondered 'why do we fall into the same trap over and over again?' ..."

This is a good question. Yet it is understandable that we will repeat our fights when we have no idea what lies behind them. We often act unconsciously and repeat unproductive patterns in attempts to get what we need.

For Z and B, communications had fallen short for so long that both were exhausted and victimised by their circumstances. Like all situations flooded by constant showers of attack and counter-attack, neither trusted the other. Fears were high, making for an escalation of pain that had up until then kept them from inspecting the site of their hurts. This meant that they never got to deal with their actual problems.

Below the surface

Working as a mediator, I have learned to look more closely at what lies behind conflict. I have learned that fear cripples creativity. I learned too that, to settle fights, we need to get beyond surfaces to what nego-tiation writers William Ury and Roger Fisher call "the interest behind the position." The phrase itself tells us that there is more to consider. We must ask what the fight is telling us.

Both experience and research have shown me that ha-bitual venting of anger can close hearts and cloud judge-ment. Rowing can become habitual, often shedding little light on how to resolve the issues. In the mediation pro-cess the details of rows are not overly dwelt upon as fu-ture behaviour is what really makes change. That said, enough time must be given so that insight is developed and settlement terms are reached.

It is important to understand what is happening for each person underneath the bubbling surface of conflict. It is important, too, that individuals understand what lies within their feelings.

To ease conflict we need to deepen our understand-ing. Mediation aims always to move from power strug-gle towards principled negotiation, where concerns are acknowledged, expressed and explored.

Beyond conflict

When working with conflict, creativity is the media-tor's lodestar. The art of the mediator is to draw out the innate creativity that is alive and well beneath the debris of conflict defences. Keeping the focus on un-furling the creative in each participant, the mediator guides beyond the fight through the changes, transitions and healing that will ease conflict. In time this will bring forward a new, more creative way of living. Understanding gives a different complexion to things. In practice I learned that there is a freshness deep in each of us that makes it possible, to start over. This is, in fact, the essence of what it means to be creative. Yet, for Z and B, easing conflict took quite some time. Some problems were tenacious. Both were very defensive to begin with. Their fears triggered forceful attempts at self-preservation. In their discussions they competed for dominance. These habits persisted for a while but, as each grew more aware of what lay behind their anger and frustration, they were more open to learning what it would take to be creative with their conflicts. Generally speaking, Z and B had been falling short of their mutual hopes for living together. Yet, as they began to understand this, they started to put their hostilities aside. When each began to believe in their ability to be creative, to believe that meeting mutual needs would require their attention, they became more hopeful about their power to make changes. Each had a lot of anger and frustrations to work through, yet over time they found a way to stay the course in learning to be more creative. Step-by-step they progressed. The bond they had as parents was never in doubt; they now had started to have a new awareness about what it takes to ease conflict. They were learning the secrets of creativity that they will inevitably model across the generations to their children. Over time it became clear that their difficulties had three main components;

1. Each held little hope that they had within themselves the ability to work things out.
2. Each was afraid and in high arousal because they felt their basic needs were being frustrated.
3. Each seemed to have difficulty respecting their differences.

It is not hard to see how, having little confidence in our problem-solving ability, fear for our basic needs and intolerance of our differences can make day-to-day creative relating a problem. During the mediation process they learned that they had within themselves the wherewithal to find solutions, that they could identify and negotiate their needs and that their differences brought potential for a creative interplay. Much of what Z and B had to learn about being creative is the subject of this book. However, the first thing they learned was that the seed of the solution lay in the problem.

The seeds of solution

The fact is that the thread running through most conflicts resonates with Z and B's main areas of complaint. Lack of awareness of our creative ability, coupled with intolerance of difference and a shortfall in basic needs for practical and emotional support, is a recipe for conflict. Yet the seed of the solution to most conflict can be found in responding to these three strands that from here on I will refer to as the *3 Essentials*.

As we incorporate these essentials in our lives we learn to respect the creative power in one another, to address needs and to honour differences. When we do we become empowered to live life to the full. Over the years the 3 *Essentials* have crystallised into the categories indicated in the diagram below.

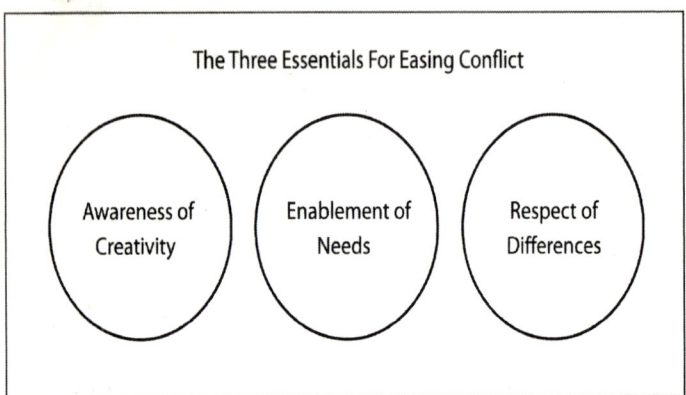

The Three Essentials For Easing Conflict

Awareness of Creativity

Enablement of Needs

Respect of Differences

Empowering all three

As we learn more about all three essentials it becomes easier to release the vitality that promotes collaboration, flexibility and a search for new solutions to life's old problems.

At their optimum, these essentials aim to activate, sustain and encourage creativity. Yes, on a day-to-day basis we all can fall short, given our feet of clay. Indeed, reality can be less than our aspirations. Yet, at such times, I can from experience recommend that there is nothing better than returning to these essentials. They can help us out of conflictual ruts and bring us back to a creative approach. They help us hold firm the belief that creativity is alive and well beyond the fallout of conflict.

If we can 'buy in' to the *3 Essentials*, we can learn what it takes to be truly creative.

Signing on for a deeper deal with creativity

Obviously there are many levels at which these essentials must get help. For instance, at a macro level they require the support of political and social structures. Yet the focus in this book is on the personal. Here, the starting power point is with each of us. This person-by-person approach to claiming our creativity may seem insignificant; yet, because most change relies on people ultimately, small changes, over time, are very powerful.

Over the course of this book I am going to highlight and reference what we need to stay creative with conflict. It is indeed an art and, like any form of art, it gets better with practice. Up front let me say that I am making a play to get your attention - I want to influence you. I want to persuade you that choosing to develop more awareness of creativity will bring ease to conflict. I am setting out to encourage possibility. To show that we can tune into our core creativity; we can balance needs and get to know that difference is the spice of life. We can each develop a creative attitude as soon as we choose. But, because generally we will change only when we believe change is possible, this is where my book can help.

Within these pages, I want to share with you the key aspects of what it will take to release creativity and ease conflict. We will begin by looking more closely at the *3 Essentials*.

PART ONE

Up Close with the 3 Essentials

CHAPTER 1
Essential 1: Creative awareness

Life-long creative inventor Buckminster Fuller warns that 'Spaceship Earth' did not arrive with a rule book. This of course honours the mystery, surprise and innovation in life. Yet we would be foolish to ignore the know-how that affirms and draws out our innate creativity.

Nature via nurture

Thankfully, these days the 'nature versus nurture' debate has moved on and emphasis is no longer on supremacy of either.

Inner and outer worlds both matter. We can honour inheritance and uniqueness and work with the realities of both. Today we know that behaviour and energy patterns can cross generations, and that genetic inheritance matters. We also know that assessing the particular mix that makes us who we are can be difficult.

In the moving picture of life, suffice it to say, experiences that shape us during the impressionable and formative years of childhood are inevitably a combination of what is innate and what comes to us with the social and cultural happenings of time and place.

Simply put, we each arrive with our own blueprint that requires certain experiences in order for us to evolve. Perhaps this is what psychologist Abraham Maslow meant when he said that, in accessing creativity, "we are not in a position in which we have nothing to work with. We already have capacities, talents, directions, missions, callings."

Alongside this, we can however say, without equivocation, that we need experiences outside ourselves to draw out and give form to our own unique essence.

Psychologist Carl Rodgers refers to personal development as "becoming that self you truly are." This inner and outer partnership can, with adequate nurturing experiences, bring out our core being. Moreover it will evolve authentically and prove more soulful than anything we might try to impose from outside.

Acknowledging this partnership is central to our well-being. Respecting individual uniqueness keeps life brimming with creative potential, while at the same time giving focus and definition to the enabling experiences we need in order to bring out our best. In the words of author Matt Ridley, it is "nature via nurture."

Personal power

The ideal of encouraging creativity is kept alive by the belief that our own unique part makes a contribution to life as a whole. Education in its original meaning holds that a wellspring at our core is where our deepest potential lies. Think of the transformation that each of us could make if we began to really trust our innate creative intelligence. We would show up with a *can do* attitude; we would bring with us a viewfinder that values drawing out the best in ourselves and in others. Collaboration would be valued beyond competition. We can 'make it together' would become our primary guiding principle.

Teachers who tread lightly and respect this individuality bring out the best in the malleable young. Freidrich Froebel, a pioneering teacher, suggested that teachers should sit quietly in the classroom and attempt to answer questions the children ask! In its earliest formulation, the term *education* implied a process of drawing out the essential essence of each individual.

When given the experiences that unfold our genuine core self, we are empowered to draw on our intrinsic creative nature. Creative nature at its deepest has a quality of oneness, binding us collectively in a great cohesive unity. In this space we all connect, no matter how tenuous that connection seems. When we stay aware of this 'depth connection', we realise that we each have a stake in the creative whole. Beyond our mood on a given day, more than our behaviour, more than the roles we play, an essential part of each one of us needs to find expression. Call it our Essence, our Divine spark, our Soul - whatever we call it, it is this Universal connectivity that unites and energises us to live fully.

We cannot relate with an attitude of creativity to others until we can connect with and understand this vital source of potential that lies within. When we respect this potential in each other, we get to author or star more fully in our own lives. Growing a sturdy self that can stay creative is a gradual matter. As we are intrinsically unique a 'one size fits all' attitude is impossible.

Speaking about temperamental differences, writer Kay Redfield Jamison tells us in her book, *Exuberance*, that some will bounce into life a little like Tigger while others are more like Piglet - slow builders. Some temperaments do favour moving slowly, gaining pace gradually. Others leap forward, eager for life. Circumstances, aptitudes and time frames differ – that's what makes us unique individuals. As adults we can indeed learn to develop a creative attitude – an attitude that values a person-centred approach. Like nature itself, we are a diverse lot. We can weave lives that run the full gamut from complex to simple, from full colour to monochrome. We can use this gift of diversity to energise and be energised, to resource and be resourced. To be truly human, we need to broaden our understanding of what it means to be creative.

Encouraging creative awareness

When we live creatively we become whole-hearted in our activities. We learn to stay centered through the phases of ebb or flow that are part of the rhythms of creativity. When we are creative we are far less likely to want to stir up trouble, we want to work things out.

Creative role models

We can observe a number of qualities in those who consistently stay creative. They work well with relationships. It might be at a domestic or global level, within a marriage or partnership, sports team or company. It matters little what the setting is because these people have one thing in common. They have learned to bring creative awareness to their relationships.

People who value creativity have their fair share of concern and challenge, yet their activities and occupations seem to engage, mobilize and harness the best in themselves and others.

They solve and resolve again and again. Their attitude is seldom one of perfectionism and they are not usually over-demanding in their approach. They seem to trust their ability to resolve difficulty and are comfortable in their own skins. They will usually be willing to show up, take a chance and express themselves. They are not easily toppled or shaken by conflict. They are realistic and see conflict is part of life. Creatively empowered people have learned to be flexible, adaptive and resourceful. They seem to have mastered the ability to cut away the extraneous and sidestep any tendency to escalate difficulty. People with an expanded sense of their creative potential find ways around obstacles and see challenge, even failure, as part of a learning curve.

It seems that such people are more connected with their true core; their authentic self. This it seems is central; and because it is, for a creative attitude to take hold, we too, need to set about connecting with our authentic core. Ideally, we best learn to be creative by having first-hand experiences of it in the company of kindred spirits. When a creative way of living is modelled, facilitated and taught, we experience it in a more heightened and real way. It is contagious, it grows and grows.

Being creatively aware will increase our chance of success in any endeavour. When we relate creatively, we can bring in timely and harmonious solutions.

Creative intelligence

To harness our creativity so that we can use it practically, will require some understanding of the emerging theories that underpin it. This takes us into tangible and non-tangible territory, what expert Deepak Chopra, who draws on the field of quantum physics, calls local and non-local intelligence. In one of his many books, *Synchro Destiny*, Dr Chopra posits that mind and body are exquisitely linked; that intent orchestrates all the creativity in the universe; and that we, as humans, are capable of creating positive changes in our lives through intent. It is, he suggests, about being open to synchronicity, the notion that we each have the power to attract what we need when we can be intentional about it and ask for it, while remaining open to receiving it. He adds that we are all born from the primal creative energy of the universe. He suggests, too, that when we are connected to our true self we have access to the creative powers of the universe. "Good luck," he says, "is opportunity and preparedness coming together. Intention will provide you with opportunity but you will still need to act when the opportunity is provided."

From this perspective we co-create our lives and give form to our ideas. Once we have a sense of this amorphous reservoir of consciousness, the pure potential that lies deep within and around each of us, we understand that we can draw on this power. This source is acknowledged by mystics and artists alike. However, connecting with a deep inner source is not only for mystics and artists, but commonplace in the intuitive leaps of scientists too. But, actually, we can all live as artists, making, shaping and contributing to life.

Without confidence in this capacity, our creative power may lie dormant. Without a belief in the deeper creative consciousness within ourselves and others, we may lower confidence in our ability to make and shape our lives. This can encourage living from surfaces rather than depths. In society, when creative attitudinal shifts reach critical mass, a powerful force for positive change can be sustained. When we take licence to live from this deeper awareness of creativity, we realise that whatever we hold strongly inside us finds expression in day-to-day living. For this reason the way we think and feel and behave is really worthy of our attention. Ask for what you need, while remembering that help given may not be all you need. Being grateful helps, for even a part of what is needed gradually builds creative momentum. We have, as humans, the gift of choice and will. By clearing what is extraneous we get to de-clutter, simplify and make plans. We get to problem-solve, make changes and learn afresh. Most problem-solving goes awry because we either flood the arena of our lives with confusions and undifferentiated intentions, or we lack openness to receive - and without that openness, our hopes cannot be realised.

When we are open to the idea that we can unfold our creativity, we can move beyond the things that hinder and into those that help us.

Openness to possibility

When we embrace a creative attitude we make things possible.

The opening lines from a poem by Emily Dickinson capture something about why possibility works: "I dwell in Possibility - A fairer House than Prose - More numerous of Windows - Superior for Doors." I was first introduced to this poem when I received a 'thank you' card from a woman who, with her partner, had stayed the course in a long process of mediating a separation agreement. The lines from *I dwell in Possibility* were on the front page. The words moved me because they were so apposite for the spirit of mediation; moreover, the woman added her heartfelt view that she would not have persevered to reach settlement if 'possibility' had not been kept alive during the mediation process.

Being open to receive what we need allows creative energy to move in a two-way process. Openness to one another enhances the qualities that let us evolve more humanly. Being open to many sources of support as we move through change will make a great difference. This helps bring what we need and will allow us to be open to giving where the needs of others, friends or family, arise, too. A two-way flow is always central in the creative process.

Openness to receive something new allows us to let go of the old and embrace the new. Solutions, opportunities and timely outcomes all depend on a willingness to be open. When we lose out on an opportunity, it is often a matter of being unwilling to be open to it.

The secondary gain of risk-free living is illusory, yet it can have us nail our boots to the floor while declaring that we like to ramble. Removing blocks and debris may be part of what we need to do to get to a more open stance. Many of us today are revisiting old wisdoms held in spiritual circles for eons, that the things that route and re-route us invite us to stay humble and accepting of the fact that we may not always see the fuller picture. This honours mystery and makes life engaging.

Engagement

Engagement requires us to clear our intention and to bring a focus to our goals. It asks us to give space over defined periods of time in order to bring about the outcomes we aim for; without genuine engagement, desired outcomes fall short. Indeed, any ongoing change will be more likely to be random and haphazard.

Intention plus focus

To become focused asks that we bring attention to the matter we are dealing with. Being focused will require us to call back our scattered energies - it asks us to be mindful. Being mindful asks us to stay in the 'here and now,' with a clear connection to our primary intention for the task in hand.

Our intention is of key importance to the energy we bring to bear on things. We can achieve success by the quality of our focused intention. That outcomes are guided by this seems fair. 'Energy follows intention' is an expression that has currency in personal growth circles. Intention is a little like a mind-set or a rule that operates as an imperative. Our intention, when clear, will guide and organize from behind the scenes. If intention is largely unconscious and negative, it will have the effect of sabotaging our more apparent conscious effort. If we have had traumatic, harsh or poor experiences, or those close to us have had them, many of our wishes and intentions may be vengeful and destructive, at worst, or disenabling, at best. Habits are strong and resistance can show up in a million disguises. Distractions and insecurities can sabotage a fuller awareness of how creative we humans truly are, and limit our spectrum.

As a mediator, some of my work will involve participants in really looking at their intention. This helps if someone has the unconscious wish to get revenge because, understandable as it may be, it will play out in negotiations and sabotage creative outcomes; energy will be placed on getting even rather than getting to solutions.

When intention for a win-win outcome is agreed, we trigger a flow of upbeat energy that ultimately shapes better outcomes. In the arts, intention sets the scene and creates the effect. *Intention* to delight is more likely to *produce* delight. If we set out to shock, to hurt, to break, we will most likely achieve it. Intentions that have no meaningful focus will lack organizing power, yet those intentions that are clear and specific will align with energy and bring results.

Time and space

Giving ourselves the time and space does wonders for easing conflict.

It helps process in organic ways the true enablers of creativity. Managing time is a big issue. When we can do this, it seems we can be more effective. As we start to make changes that will ease conflict we may need to put effort into factoring in time for reflection.

Time perspectives depend on the goals people have. Artists may need a lot of 'mooching' time to incubate ideas. Parents need 'slow time' to be available to their children. Businesses need to measure and cost time, and so on. When we value time we are time-conscious; we may structure time, take time, give time, allow time and enjoy time. The wry and highly industrious French writer Colette, when speaking of her daughter, said "she consumes time without employing it!" Constant 'busy-ness' can make it hard to leave space for reflection. Down time is good for us. It is a useful foil for effort and productivity.

There is nothing so harrowing and energy-draining as living on a treadmill; in the speediness of life today, it can be difficult to spare time for the reflection that is part of our healing challenge; yet, getting the habit of consciously managing time will be part of what personal growth in creativity will ask of us. Keeping track and pace in our process of change will help us to be successful.

We see examples of how easing conflict can be postponed by distraction and 'busy-ness,' but when the behaviour becomes addictive and compulsive we are in danger of compounding our problems. When we are at our most creative it seems we are willing to move in rhythms of both active and fallow; stepping out and stepping back. In this rhythmic dance we carry on our relationships, shaping the stuff that forms the everyday tasks that make our futures. This way we require less energy for better results. Wu Wei, the ancient Chinese tradition, called it the path of least resistance and it is expressed in folksy terms as to do without striving so everything gets done. To make changes we need time to reflect, observe, and take stock. Blaise Pascal, the French philosopher and physicist, once said that "all man's miseries derive from not being able to sit quietly in a room alone". Allowing time so that the changes we make can mature and take hold is important. Any change process requires time for the new to bed in and assimilate. Being time-aware we can employ our time more consciously. Using time consciously will make us more mindful.

Mindfulness

Mindfulness is a teaching that philosophers and mystics alike have held sacred through the ages. It is a condition that keeps us fresh, steady and alert. In mindfulness we can stay in the moment, reinterpret, reinvent. In her book, *On Becoming an Artist,* Ellen J. Langer says:

"mindfulness is a natural partner of creativity ... when we are mindful we are centered, and of course this is where we would prefer to be. But social situations can be so complex that we often get thrown off our centre and don't recognise it. We get caught in a script that dictates how we think we should behave ... we get pulled in, becoming reactive rather than active. 'I said this because he said that.' We give up control over our behaviour and emotions. At this point, we are even more likely to play out a mindless script that tells us how we should think, act and feel. Later we may say that the other person pressed our buttons, as if the interaction could not have taken a different turn. Of course we could have chosen to do otherwise if we were in the present to make the choice. The more mindful we are, the more choices we have and the less reactive we become. We don't realise when we are mindless. We are not there to notice."

Most of us have difficulty with *mindfulness* in the complexity of life today. Yet we can gradually reclaim it as we begin to value its importance to creativity.

A process of gradual progress

When we connect creatively with life we develop a flexible attitude and we take a process approach to it.

Creativity invites us to trust, to start over again on a daily and regular basis, to stay fresh in our approach. It asks us to stay cool and to take progressive steps. Being creative is not necessarily about mastery or any given outcome. It is not about living free from future hassles or 'happily ever after.' It is a way of relating that requires us to open our minds to possibility and discovery.

It asks us to believe that we cannot know the outcome from the outset. It asks us to prepare for success and to weather failures. In much the same way as the potter hands over her pot to the kiln, having done her part, we get used to doing our part and letting go. Like the potter we will have trials and errors as we learn, yet as we get skilled, we will have good outcomes and cool surprises. When we are in flow with our ability to be creative we are drawn along in our endeavours; outcomes are often better than we expected. We learn that what we call failures are only feedbacks that can challenge and re-route us to learn something new. We learn to discriminate, to gain greater flexibility. We learn to forget our naysaying, sidestep misery, get out of the rut of fear-based conflicts and get into the groove of promoting the trust that empowers creativity. As we learn to release our creative potential, growth and expansion in keeping with our own unique self becomes a reality. We can take paths that map our life and make our unique, authentic contribution. We can put ourselves into relationships and situations where we aim to be broad and genuine. We can sniff out the real and worthwhile and focus our energy on doing our best. The experiences that lead to our creative awakening can then become part of the rich reservoir of social experience. It can be passed on to help promote creativity in ever-widening circles. When our own pebble drops, it ripples out.

We will revisit creative awareness again with a view to reclaiming our natural aptitude for it. We will see how we can foster it anew. Next however, with Essential 2, we will begin to learn how the common needs index we each share is the key to releasing creativity. These needs have been the focus of psychologists, researchers and practitioners for the last century. It is now generally accepted that optimal levels of the following experiences can activate enable and sustain individuals to release their creative power. We learn that our most creative nature is released with a helping hand. We move towards what it takes to empower it.

THE ART OF EASING CONFLICT

CHAPTER 2
ESSENTIAL 2: ENABLING OUR NEEDS

A helping hand

Today we can draw on the work of psychologists like Maslow, Eriksson, Jung and Rodgers, who have forged ideas and given us insights. Their writings have mined seams of gold and little gems to help make life richer. Looking over their body of work, we find re-takes on the great noble aspirations for humanity that are inherent in cultures around the world. The experiences we need to help us develop and sustain creativity are universal and essentially democratic, and they can be found in ancient cultural wisdoms. Eastern and Western philosophy has been an inspiration for modern psychologists who are engaged in helping us to expand and grapple with the complexity of living well in a global environment. In practice, we are enabled to be creative with a combination of know-how, emotional support and material help. We cannot come truly into sustainable creativity until we can adequately meet our need to be safely nourished, respected and empowered. This being the case, we must bring a whole-hearted approach to the task of accessing our needs. These are primal and common to people the world over; moreover, meeting these needs is a challenge for each generation.

Psychologist Abraham Maslow, helpfully and simply, outlined a pyramid of needs that provide a pathway to creativity in human development. These, he claimed, are the building blocks that help us access our most creative nature in incremental steps. See Diagram below:

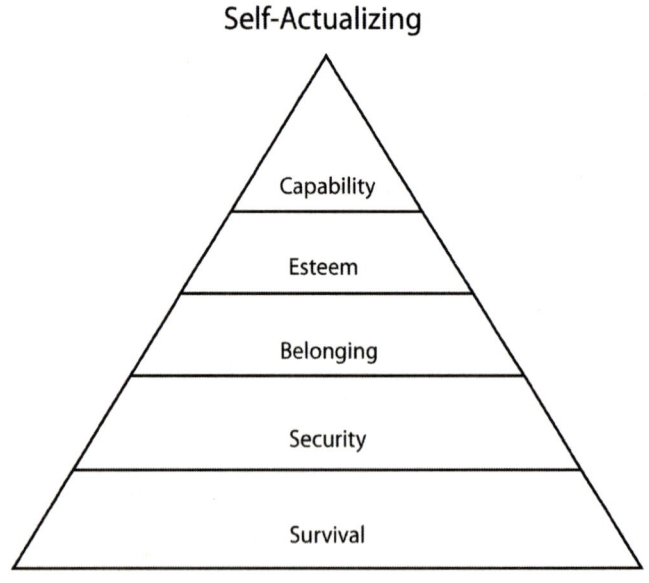

Self-Actualizing

Capability

Esteem

Belonging

Security

Survival

Maslow Hierarchy of Needs

BASED ON: A.H MASLOW'S, A HIERACHY OF BASIC NEEDS.MOTIVATION AND PERSONALITY, HARPER & ROW NEW YORK 1970

Maslow believed that this hierarchy of needs builds one on another and, when experienced to an optimal level, allows each of us to reach the apex. For Maslow, the apex represented a state he called 'self-actualizing.' When we achieve optimal levels in all five, Maslow believed that we can be creative in ongoing cycles throughout our lives – here is a snapshot of his teaching, expanded on later.

Level 1 - *Survival*

When our basic nurture needs are met, we have the energy we need to survive. When we are nourished regularly and sheltered well in infancy and, indeed, throughout life, the basic foundations for loving bonds and attachments are formed. Nurturing enables 'give and take,' and teaches us to pass on nurture by sharing.

Level 2 - *Security*

When healthy levels of nurture are sustained over time, the growing person learns to feel safe and secure. When we get to feel secure we can both take a risk and be protective. In this way we develop healthy limits.

Level 3 *Belonging*

When we can make connections and stand apart, we are able to experience a healthy sense of belonging. For instance, as we are by our nature interrelated beings, not islands, we need to be part of a network as we go about the activities of our lives.

Level 4 *Esteem*

Within our family, when we are given the message that we are worthwhile, respected and valued for our essential self, our self-esteem grows. Being valued for our authentic self, for being a person in our own right; loved for who we are, not what we do, is the foundation of self-worth.

Level 5 - *Capability*

As individuals, we acquire capability when both our inner aptitude and the skills we need for authentic self expression are developed. Over time we learn to trust this partnering and with it we can be expressive in ongoing cycles throughout our lifespan.

Activating our creativity

When we achieve such optimal levels in all five, Maslow suggested that we become 'self-actualising'. Someone who achieves this state, Maslow believed, would be creative in renewable cycles. And, because to be creative is to be naturally dynamic, there is no fixed state of being self- actualized.

I have dubbed Maslow's needs pyramid, the *5 Enablers,* because they are so central in enabling creativity. They are the developmental experiences that make it possible to use and promote our innate creativity.

Sustaining life

To use our core creativity so that we stay artful with conflict will mean becoming *au fait* with all 5 *Enablers.* These are the spectrum of enabling experiences that will encourage the flow of creativity in very practical ways. Because each level of experience provides us with a variety of human attributes, as such they are the life-giving qualities we need in order to first use, and then pass on. Taken together, they translate to life skills that are the hallmarks of sustainable living.

These experiences are regular and ordinary, and repeated over time, they give us all we need in order to stay creative. Yet huge numbers of people currently miss out on having optimal levels in these most formative needs.

This vital life-enhancing mix, provides the qualities that make or break our ability to be flexible, collaborative and hopeful; the very essence of creativity.

Needs enablement

These are the qualities that mastermind the easing of conflict. And they are simple enough, given encouragement. For instance when well-grounded, they will give us the ability to share, to explore, to value, to participate and to express in an authentic way. Without some understanding of the role of the *5 Enablers*, mastering the art of easing conflict can be difficult. The often overwhelming numbers of stimuli that we meet day to day in our lives can benefit from having a meaningful framework, especially when the going gets tough.

In every transaction of our lives we are seeking to secure our survival and integrity. Fears about losing out on needs affect us deeply, limiting our ability to be flexible, resilient and ultimately, creative - sabotaging and stunting progress. Conversely, when we know what we need and trust that we have what it takes to negotiate our needs, we can prevent 'overheating' when tensions rise and conflict comes to call. When fear around need abounds, it sets in train behaviour that seeks to create external 'power over' given situations. This moves us away from the internal integrity power that flows from having a connection with our creative core. When power over something hardens into control patterns, personal empowerment is diminished, and with it goes sustainable creativity.

When we relate creatively we can bring in timely solutions. We will begin to see a little later how our experiences in each augment, circle and strengthen the other for better or worse.

We are already 'hard-wired' for creativity to flow. Yet we need experiences that affirm, activate and release it.

When we achieve these with even a modicum of success we begin to come into our creative power. We begin to individuate and allow others the same privilege. We learn to leave the familiar and deal with challenges, without being toppled by them. Indeed, the very opposite happens; we begin to relish and delight in new challenge. When we can integrate these experiences, we can thrive - you might say we get enabled to the power of five! Taken in the round, they can help to shape sturdy, flexible people. Maslow's pyramid of needs is used widely by people in business, education, social work and psychology. They are readily understood and can help build the structures that support the flow of creativity. Given the dynamic nature of life, we of course regularly have to update, sustain and build on the *5 Enablers* so learning to know what they are and when our baseline experience in each is being adequately met, is an ongoing life task. These 5 *Enablers* underpin the aspirations enshrined in charters and constitutions of human rights for individuals. Indeed it is deficits in these needs that fuel most human conflicts. Because they are key formative experiences, seeking out these needs is primal and meeting them, as we will see again in more detail later in part three, is central to conflict resolution.

When we truly understand the enormous potential that can come about with awareness of these needs, it spurs us to make them a priority.

CHAPTER 3
MORE ON NEEDS ENABLEMENT

Circles and spirals

Although presented by Maslow in a block-building fashion, in practice these needs regularly overlap. They are the experiences that require a constant focus and generally must be met in age-appropriate ways. Together they have a circulating and interdependent quality - gaps in one area affect other areas just as success in one area creates optimal conditions for success in others. These experiences join up, coalesce and strengthen each other, drawing up and out the very best in us.

Enabling resources

Any relationship offers an opportunity for the enabling experiences that resource us. Importantly the type of parenting we receive has an impact in early childhood when dependency is high. Later supports, like schooling, role models and friendships all play a role in giving the experiences that activate creativity.

The poet Walt Whitman captures the power of childhood experience in the lines below:

There was a child went forth every day;

And the first object he look'd upon, that object he became;

And that object became part of him for the day, or a certain part of the day, or for many years, or stretching cycles of years.

The range of resources, flexibility and skill needed to give safe passage to a child through the normal developmental stages of their life is very wide. Children go forward and regress, growing and accumulating the experiences they need to reach maturity. In the web of supports, cross-fertilizations and challenges, all families go through this process as they mature. Experiences help shape, draw out, and develop us, as we move through life. The skill, know-how and emotional support we need to deal with challenges must be sourced and harnessed. When we are resourced we make and shape the things we need and desire. With resources we can live fruitful and productive lives. Resources run the full gamut from our most basic requirements to the more sophisticated techniques we need to bring ideas into form. At every stage of life we need to have resources at the ready. We need to seek them out and be receptive to accepting those that are applicable to each specific challenge.

Under-resourcing often means that potential will not be realised.

Meeting our needs

To simply clarify the experiences we need to unfurl our innate creativity, I will spotlight each experience individually. In the diagram below each is represented as a digit;

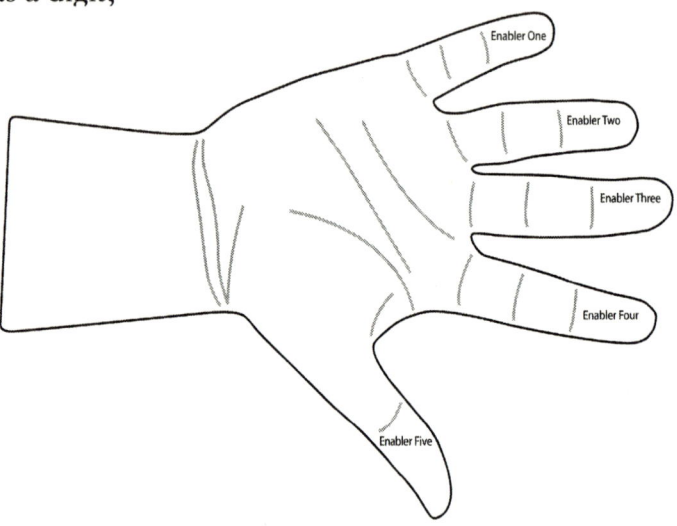

Spotlight on the 5 *Enablers*

The 5 *Enablers* speak to needs that are universal, yet particular to each of us. When encouraged, activated and supported, they build the essentials that bring forward our truest self - the self that, by its very nature, is part of what links us to the wider creative collective. This is what lets us co-operate and feel connection with others in a way that honours our holistic make-up. The essentials add up and switch us on to our own - and others' - creativity, allowing us to live life to the full.

Enabler 1 - The experience of *Survival*

Around the world in family circles children are nurtured so that they can survive, thrive and pass on energy to the next generation. Children need to be nurtured; for well-being they need food, shelter, touch and warmth.

A regular, reliable baseline in each of these needs lets a child grow strong. Our first experience of family life has huge power over our well-being. When we are young we are totally reliant on our family for care, so that when we need our family we go to great lengths to gain approval and remain within the family structure. Nature designed it that way. It is primal. Babies have been equipped with a cry that is quite intolerable to listen to for this very reason: It lets those nearby know that they need attention. There is no getting away from the fact that the care we get as growing children forms the energy that allows us to develop and evolve. Having contact, being held warmly, being housed and fed are essential to our survival. Being put outside one's family is experienced as abandonment. For a young child this could be tantamount to death.

Enabler 2 - The experience of *Security*

Developmentally, the process of feeling secure begins early in life. It is affected by the level of safety and challenge in the environment in which we find ourselves. Learning to feel secure is a developmental task that teaches healthy trust. We learn healthy levels of trust by having age-appropriate experiences that give us challenge yet provide protection.

We need support that gives protective boundaries. We need challenges that will help break down experiences into manageable size. Both risk and protection, therefore, are essential to stretch us and help provide the containment that prevents us from being overwhelmed. Opportunity to risk and build resilience is an essential part of childhood. Small sequential steps build. We get to keep our instincts in good working order so that we can challenge our limits in healthy ways while staying alert to real danger. Supports that are protective must work in tandem with the aim for risk and resilience.

All civilized societies take child protection seriously. Protection of boundary invasion in children is so important, because trauma can scar and debilitate for life. The more evolved we become, the more we recognise that protection of children is the essence of what makes a caring society. By having trustworthy experiences we learn to act in ways that are trustworthy for ourselves and for others.

We need to understand that learning to 'dance' between risk and security is a gradual and specific process.

Learning to practice courage and optimism in the face of failures, to dust ourselves off and start again, are practices that sustain progress. Childhood begins this process and our security index is informed in our families. Role models help us learn easily and naturally; they are of vital importance because they influence our trust levels for better or worse. Our care-giver's own personal experience of trust matters; their own level of trust is a powerful determinant, as habits can cross generations.

Enabler 3 - The experience of *Belonging*

The family is our primary group. Being part of a family when we are young has a quality of merging. Identification with family is high. Because of this there is no group in the world that will exert as great a feeling of pressure to belong as that of our family of origin. Belonging first takes place in the bodies of our mothers and from conception creates our experience of containment. After birth, the family is where we experience the feeling of being involved, being part of a group.

The experience of belonging is always at play in the human condition. This is the experience of both "making a connection" and of "standing alone". Merging and moving away form the first two-step dance of our existence. It has a movement that resonates with holding on and letting go. It lets us make connections and experience our common humanity, and also allows us to stand apart and experience ourselves as separate.

As an experience, its movement constantly taps out the patterns of all life's relationships. Inter-relationship is integral to living. It is our inherent nature to want to associate, to trade and co-create - in fact, our very survival depends on it. As we learn and become seasoned, we develop a readiness to meet and explore the world in all its diversity. We learn to live autonomously, equipped for both connection and separateness. It is not hard to see how important it is for us to become seasoned at both. Ultimately, our ability to handle each makes or breaks our ability with negotiation. Success with negotiation is forged in a climate that gives opportunity for both connection and separateness.

No-one is an island; we are relational in our nature. Group life is part of us and, within the group, we engage in cross-fertilizing, exchanging, and living. It is little wonder that belonging in the family of origin is said to be non-negotiable. It gives us our first taste of inclusion and participation. At its optimum, belonging is all about being part of a group. When we belong, we develop a sense of having a touchstone, roots and a reference point.

When we are healthy, even as a young child, we will gradually move to wider and more diverse groups, reflecting our growing need for expansion.

The bonds formed in earliest belonging experiences can be replicated when we make forays into new surroundings. Later, as individuals, we naturally belong to diverse groups as we organize our life and work patterns.

Healthy belonging lets us take, and fill, our space. It asks that we let others do the same. We become part of a sharing network. It asks for participation and it gives identity. We come together to build teams and give form to dreams.

Enabler 4 - The experience of *Esteem*

Being validated, mirrored and empathised with are the experiences that make self- esteem. Self-esteem is nothing to do with being perfect. In fact, perfectionism often springs from low self-esteem or feelings of shame and can be the greatest hindrance to connecting with our creative self. Realness is born out of clarity about self - it is born out of knowing our strengths and our limits.

It's little wonder that many of us struggle with self-esteem and personal empowerment issues when we are fed scripts that discourage trusting or using our deep connection to our core self. Facilitating the true self doesn't preclude setting limits or challenging oneself. It does, however, require respectful recognition of each individual's uniqueness. This inner creative source, that can contribute so much, seems to present a great challenge for many systems. Our innate authentic flairs light the way and shape our personalities. We follow and commit ourselves deeply to what draws us. We enter relationships and live true to our inner wisdom.

Tapping to our own 'music' and letting it resonate with others is both gift and challenge. That we are each unique and have our own particular gifts and limits is a given. However, valuing and owning this notion for ourselves and others is sometimes not as well affirmed as it might be. We are today bombarded with the neatly-packaged images in the media showing advertisements about what makes us worth it; the reality of a more true self may not meet with manipulated images. Recently I heard the term 'contingent self-esteem.' Loosely, it refers to the idea that we are valued and esteemed depending on our achievements only. Fair and well for developing skill in some situations, however, at a deeper level in personal development, it misses the point that human value is an inherent right.

Trusting the creative power that lies in the deep intuitive core of each of us can be hard, particularly in climates where the rational is promoted to excess. The belief that the inner core self is deeply wise, and a more vital guide to success than anything imposed from outside, is not only sustainable but is now well supported in fields of psychology and education. With self-esteem we can be authentic. Being authentic asks us to be honest, while to be real asks us to be genuine; it also asks that we can value strengths and accept, or work with, shortcomings.

Self-esteem lets us be autonomous and, when we are, we remain tuned to our ability to think, feel, intuit, sense and perceive. We can take responsibility for our behaviour and be a team player. To be autonomous need never be mistaken for being selfish and confers no right to be self-obsessed. In fact, when we gain self-knowledge we know our core self we can live more compassionately, taking on board the strengths and shortfalls of ourselves and of others. When our self-esteem is intact, we have a connection with our truly dynamic self. We are not seeking a once and for all fixed self but, instead, a capacity to stay aware and connected with our true evolving potential. The multi-faceted dimension of selfhood suggests that like a diamond different aspects get to sparkle in differing circumstances. It seems that we must have encouragement in order to be authentic and real in the various circumstances and configurations of our personalities.

During our childhood, we need a deep and staunch connection with our carers. To develop sufficient self-esteem we need relationship; we need to be encouraged in our relationship to be real and we need our realness to matter. Growing children have a primary need to be respected for themselves, to have their own thoughts and emotions and aspirations validated - something psychologists call a 'narcissistic need.' If we are deprived of this naturally arising need during our formative years we may spend enormous energy attempting to pull parents or parent substitutes into our lives to meet it. When we are acting out unmet healthy childhood 'narcissistic needs,' our creative energy is trapped at immature levels.

Self-esteem has an unconditional quality in that it is not based on our achievements. At its purest, how valuable, or how lovable, we are is not conditional on good days or bad days. Relationships act like a mirror and can reflect acceptance and affirmation of our authentic self within the bounds of healthy limits. At its most aspirational, a soulful passage through natural healthy narcissistic phases involves love, constancy and honesty. These are core needs - when they are met, we grow sturdy. For instance, when children, with their full range of quirks and qualities, perceive themselves as being loved, they learn to experience themselves as loveable.

When we are valued we are empowered; we live by the rule that we can have input into the design of our lives. We can say, I need, I can, I will, I won't. In other words, we can assert ourselves. We believe our needs are valuable. We can know the full range of experience - cognitive, sensory and affective. We sense what is going on. What we feel, what we are touching. We can think and we can negotiate.

We learn to value ourselves when we have experiences that say we are worthwhile and lovable. When a parent or trusted adult spends time listening and talking with a child, and when the child's view and opinion is valued, affirmed or talked through, and their wishes and hopes are held to be important - then a child will know they are valued. When those who care for us during our formative years make connections that confirm the good in us, we learn that we are worthwhile – it is in this experience that the development of self-esteem happens. This is the experience that allows one to attract love and to recognise when they are encountering something else.

These kinds of experience develop feelings of esteem that help us to value our inherent worth. When we encounter ourselves in totality, warts and all, we will be on our way to developing healthy self-esteem.

With true self-esteem we are comfortable in our own skin and are more likely to esteem others. This is the foundation stone of mutual respect and paves the way for co-operation. Having good self-esteem is central to healthy creativity.

Enabler 5 - The experience of *Capability*

Becoming capable is about realizing potential through learning self-discipline, responsibility and confidence. Together, these are acknowledged as so basic to having a happy creative life that education as a system has become an institutional force in society.

No one family can provide the range of learning needed. At its most aspirational, education generally sets itself the task of developing capable and responsible people, while keeping in mind the need a healthy child has to be authentic and autonomous. Becoming authentic by and large means unfolding, expressing and being true to our genuine potential.

Potential is drawn out throughout our developing years in age-appropriate ways, The task of all education is to draw out the best in each personality. From this perspective we can learn to know and express ourselves more truly.

Where education empowers individuals, they are not capable of following blindly and are more defiant of dictates that jar with individual creative power.

Children learn to be capable when given structures that help them learn. They need instructions as well as time to learn. When they are allowed time to learn, to practice and to make mistakes, they become capable.

Ideally, as their own particular learning style and attitudes are encouraged, they can learn well. The temperament of a child does play an interacting part in how well they learn. Temperament usually refers to the range of characteristics that include energy levels, ability to adjust or modulate feelings, sensitivity to sights, sounds and other stimuli.

Some children present as being more tenacious, sensitive, intense or adaptive, and all of these need to be considered. Children easily become responsible when they live in circumstances where responsibility is respected and modelled. Being responsible will involve being mindful enough to respect your own and other people's well-being and property. Play is one of the best ways to promote learning; both children and adults generally thrive when play-centered learning can be achieved. Having the discipline and commitment to teach children how to learn is indeed challenging, painstaking though it is, yet so totally rewarding when we see them bring their ideas into form.

Schooling, when it works well, can build levels of confidence that, while as we saw earlier, this alone is not sufficient to build self-esteem, can bolster it. Sadly, where schooling is poor it can do harm to self-esteem. This can mean disempowerment, drop-out and even marginalization if a child reacts by detaching. When children become detached they are at risk to a whole range of harmful knock-on effects, ranging from aggression to depression. Learning and exploring the best way to handle the care role is, therefore, an extremely interesting and challenging task. When this happens, children become capable.

As their efforts are praised and rewarded, they remain encouraged, experiencing growing capability.

Optimal conditions

As noted, flexibility in all *5 Enablers* is learned in the rhythmic movements that begin in early life, allowing each of us to progress in what seem like paradoxical childhood developmental tasks. It seems we learn from opposite experiences, some that hold us and some that challenge us, until healthy balance is reached. Both types of experiences are necessary because both have value. For instance, a good age-appropriate challenge helps one learn independence, while support builds a willingness to receive help from others. By a combination of both inner and outer support we pace and trace the rhythms and paths of our lives.

Development of flexibility mostly works in combinations of challenge and support. When we have support, challenge and openness to learning, we can unfurl our creative nature. As we do, we get the flexibility that helps us deal with life in all its diverse complexity. We get all, or at least some, of these supports and challenges in incremental ways from our families, teachers, colleagues and friends, in our homes, schools, work settings and communities.

To reach maturity, capable of making our way in a complex and increasingly global world requires the purposeful and enabling steps set out above. These five enablers are formative during childhood. We know that the young are porous and malleable, which means they are dependent and impressionable during their early years. To a large degree, the experiences and consequent attitudes, habits and patterns begin to take shape during these malleable years of childhood. Unsurprisingly then, childhood is the ideal and optimal time to learn.

Ideally in situations unhampered by major distress or trauma, such experiences are learned naturally and easily, and are passed on across generations in ways that are generally good enough.

With an optimal mix of the 5 *Enablers*, real and sustainable creative power is sourced and activated. As adults, this is an individual matter and change is only sustainable with our own co-operation. Throughout our lives we engage in this creative unfurling, moving in and out, in a diverse world. Within this diversity we make connections and pattern our lives. Because experiences are often less than ideal (and, in truth, few situations are without flaw) many of us may experience imbalances around needs. We will, as I have said, come back to the task of balancing these needs in Part Two. However, for now, we can move to the third essential, that is the importance of honouring difference. We will see how understanding differences is central when we aim to live creatively and bring ease to conflict.

CHAPTER 4
ESSENTIAL 3: RESPECT
OF DIFFERENCE

When a Frenchman during a gender debate quipped, "*Vive la différence,*" its tone had a celebratory note and the ring of a truism. That difference is real and here to stay is certain. Moreover, difference is essential.

Letting difference be, or, indeed embracing and celebrating it, is the aim of all genuine liberals. Most of us know that forcing uniformity in any situation may be convenient but inevitably it strikes a fatal blow to creativity.

Attempting to limit complexity to 'one size fits all' may seem like a way of reducing tension but, like anything forced, it has a way of rebounding with equal ferocity. Difference occurs in small and big ways in the course of living. Hundreds, perhaps thousands, of times every day we select, either consciously or unconsciously, how we relate to the differences that show up in the happenstance of our lives. When we can value and include difference we have the makings of a rich and varied life, a little like making a tapestry where differing strands add tone and contrast.

Inclusiveness / inter-relatedness

Including difference goes to the very core of the creative process.

As we have seen, to ground the five enablers will give us the power that honours the reality that we are inextricably linked in humanity with all its conundrums. When we let ourselves be dynamic, live in the possibility that we can meet our needs and heal life's hurts, the hook of absolute positions about right-doing and wrong-doing has little attraction. Lao Tzu, the father of Taoism, tells us that the wise disregard the absolute:

"... For among the creatures of the world some go in front and some follow; some blow hot when others would be blowing cold. Some are feeling vigorous just when others are worn out. Some are loading just when others are tilting out ..."

In this frame of mind, we make space for learning to recognise and contribute to the fascination and wonder of diversity that creates lifes variety. We move off fixed positions and make possible the conditions for problem-solving and innovation. We learn to move beyond problems to collaboration and resolve - beyond conflicts - to acceptance of differences.

Live and let live

We have an essential nature that connects us, making us interdependent and co -evolving.

We sometimes have to dig deeper to get to our common ground, to find what binds us, rather than what separates us.

When we begin to accept ourselves as part of nature, we also understand that we are bound by what is essentially an organic nature. No equivocation is possible on this. Difference is part and parcel of our blueprint.

We must learn to be comfortable in a 'live and let live' culture. To get along we have to engage, respect and tolerate talking through our respective needs. To mature through our growth needs is to grow into our creative best. From an attitude of understanding our own needs and those of others we get to know what makes us tick - we learn the pieces we find comfortable and those we are slower to embrace, the strengths each one of us has and those we lack. When we get to see the full picture we get a wider perspective and are less prone to waste energy or to blame and fight with others.

Our generation is entering differing times and is communicating from information and circumstances which were not available to previous generations. Living today has challenges so we must learn how to approach difference harmoniously. The painter Robert Rauchenberg has said: "It would be a very fine thing if people would realize that all they had in common is their difference."

To be creative we need to live and work in this spirit. To maintain harmony with each other we need to co-operate. We need to be stress-hardy, capable and energetic in the face of difference. When healthy, we understand that harmony is not brought about by force and domination in an organic system. When we can ride out the tension and stress we are free to visualize and embrace possibility and opportunity. Our dealings with difference then become successful, collaborative and full of upbeat energy. Living this way we work together and tackle the challenge of being human.

Understanding everyday differences

As individuals, we are operating in a diverse and changing environment. Putting difference together in new forms to surprise and innovate is the stuff of creativity. Combining and balancing difference, we stimulate new ideas to create change and possibility. When we begin to view difference as the raw material and impetus for change, growth and possibility, we enable progress and alter our way of relating to it. This natural tendency to use difference to complement or stimulate will let us cross-fertilize, expand, change and grow. It begs to flourish and is a nature so powerful that, when repressed, can leave us feeling 'soul-sick.' Eventually, repression will lead to frustration and blockage.

Common bonds

Understandably, we can feel very comfortable when we bond through a sense of sameness. Our similarities let us merge and lull us into a feeling of security and togetherness. Co-operation feels easier where commonality is the norm. Of course, the deeper reality is that we are bound by our common humanity, but bonds for many have been severely challenged over time.

Where we find difference exciting, manageable or complementary, we are invigorated. This is particularly true when some obvious similarities or common views help hold a connection while we navigate our differences. However, beyond our comfort zones many of us may find difference much trickier. Gaps in understanding can make bridging our differences harder. The wider we perceive the gap to be, the greater the scope for rising tensions. In the gap we can easily exclude others; we may stereotype, dismiss and offend, making it more likely that we will incite conflict.

We regularly deal with mismatch of difference in our families, at work and in wider community circles. Difference in values, personal attributes, resources and timing are widespread. Difference can be concrete or intangible, and mismatches or inequality often lead to jealousy and struggle. Wars have been fought to possess or dispossess, and to homogenise difference with tragic consequences that carry through the ages. Differences are always interacting and playing out in the drama of life. Creatively harmonising difference will ask us to build trust. Below are some of the everyday differences that speckle our existence. In their differing strands, they weave the complex patterns in our lives. They can be grouped like this:

Cultural values

In the richness of cultural diversity we cross-fertilize our collective creativity. When it works well it is complementary and brings expansion and peace. Yet, as we know, there is potential for more heat than light when people get going on the subject of values and culture. Subjects like religion, history and politics are often avoided assiduously to prevent arousal or clash between people of differing beliefs or standards.

The current attempt to create politically correct environments is a bid to promote a 'live and let live' climate. Without savvy or care, passion can overshadow reason, leading to the insults that hurt human decency. A recent study on diversity by American sociologist Robert Putnam elaborates on the term 'social capital.' Defining it as the capacity to network with trust and mutuality, he raises one of the challenges in today's world – that is how our society can go about creating a greater sense of 'we' ? How can we move beyond the old assimilation idea of making 'them' like 'us' to a more pluralist society?

Putnam refers to a worrying phenomenon that he dubs 'hunkering down.' He describes it as a bit like the way a turtle pulls in his neck. It is common to all of us yet, at a time when the world has entered a multiethnic development phase, this raises concerns about trends of social withdrawal into multi-racial insularity. Being cut off, we find it hard to bridge differences. When we have no bridges and common projects, it becomes easier to project imagined dangers. Trust, as I will elaborate later encourages us to share, explore, participate, value and express which are all key to creativity, fears are associated with the kind of shut down or attack that add fuel to conflicts.

Immigration and diversity are good for us, associated as they are with expanding ideas and understanding, complementing growth in economies. Yet we must be willing to have shared exchanges with security, respect, inclusiveness and to encourage expression for all groups if we are to create the fair balances that build trust. We will benefit from ground rules and legislation where they enshrine basic humanitarian needs.

Biological endowment

We are innately endowed with many energy differences.

Take the differences that exist between the sexes for instance. This might well be called the master difference, as it is fundamental to the basic unit of existence. At its best, the frisson and tension of this inter-relationship is life sustaining, energising and productive. Yet the ongoing politics of gender difference is sometimes referred to as 'the longest war.' The dance of difference is experienced so acutely, that some are prompted to ask if men and women come from the same planet! There is no difference that requires more careful mediating so that respect for natural balance is maintained.

These are times where equality between the sexes begs careful negotiation. Harmonising difference asks that we move off any tendency towards demeaning either gender because it creates dangerous levels of disempowerment. The oft-quoted title of John Gray's *Men are from Mars, Women are from Venus* is catchy but implies that one gender loves while the other goes to war, so it might not be the whole picture. Domination or subjugation of either sex distorts and destroys creativity. Both masculine and feminine qualities reside in all of us, so developing and respecting both aspects is essential in any creative process. Developing the strengths of both within ourselves can help us to be flexible and resilient.

Moreover, we are all individual; it is a given - now how complex is that? Differences vary too in the levels of sensibility, resilience and strength that we have. This plays a strong role in wellbeing. Health is acknowledged as the greatest source of empowerment because ill health reduces our energy, cuts down our vitality and causes us to fare less well. Nature plus nurture variations create even further differences. For most, our genetic inheritance bestows both strengths and vulnerabilities. In nurture terms also we find differences. What sociologists call 'cumulative advantage' can mean that resources, too, will ultimately cluster, letting the well endowed have advantage and bolstering the excuse throughout time that the poor will always be with us.

Cycles, rhythms, change

The rhythms and cycles of time affect energy and opportunity too. Timing mismatches can crop up in any situation putting us out of sync. The Greek philosopher Heraclitus suggested flux and change is our only certainty. This means that life evolves and that change, in itself, is creating differences we have to deal with. Knowing when to go into action and when to stay still is a subtle art. Is it time to plant or harvest? Is it time to leave or arrive?

Our life cycles bring the opportunity and challenge of differing needs and interests. The needs of the elderly differ from those of children and so on. Skateboarders must respect the zimmer frame user and the zimmer user, the skateboarder! Cross-generational stress needs constant navigation - the balance of needs must be genuinely addressed. In my work as a mediator I regularly meet people caught up in conflicts where the competing needs of three generations are at play. Grandmother may have time on her hands - lonely perhaps. Young parents have no time - their work schedule too busy. The demands of children cannot be deferred so negotiating can be challenging.

By even contemplating the broad definitions of differences, we can see how this opens the way for mismatch and misunderstanding.. Differences create divisions in approaches and variety in outcomes. Indeed differences are often hotly debated in family and workplace alike.

Clued-in and observant of the power of differences, we can check in and learn to work with them.

Difficulty with difference

The fact is, however, that we learn more from our differences than from our similarities. Sadly, many of us respond to the challenge of difference with avoidance or opposition. Yet we have to stay with differences, and rise to this challenge in order to grow and to create in fresh and healthy ways. New learning as a concept asks us to move away from the familiar; in spite of its popularity as a theory, in practice it asks us to move from the known to the unknown, so it can feel really challenging.

The young love the feeling of merging - the sense of sameness; while real maturity asks us to respect and embrace - and even delight in difference. Difference in others is not the problem but our responses can be. Now, more than at any other time in history, learning to get along and value diversity is of supreme importance. This said, it in no way denies that valuing, embracing, even just tolerating the tensions of difference can indeed be challenging at whatever level we encounter it, in the family, the workplace, the community or at national level.

Living anywhere today has international flavour. In London there are as many as two hundred languages spoken. We must dig deep to achieve understanding. Ireland, the country in which I live, has moved in recent years from being mono-cultural to multicultural. The change has been rapid and, although essentially friendly, people in general are quick to worry about being overwhelmed. Needless to say, where fair principles are enshrined, peace blooms quickest. With respect for difference we have the mix that lets us do magic with contrasts; without respect for differences, interactions can take on an oppositional quality that attracts conflict and becomes exhausting. When we learn that to embrace diversity is the gateway to enhanced creativity, we will begin to develop the insights that let us juxtapose difference, and make new effective life patterns. More understanding of the value of difference and of how drawing out our natural creativity helps give us the stress-hardiness we need to weather the tensions that differences can generate. Embracing diversity is what will ease the situation. The human need to connect, relate and express never goes away. Discussing with each other, broadening our approach and understanding, is how we make a start. Becoming resilient with differences, expecting them, honouring them and accepting them, is what we can learn to do.

We will begin to discern the smart attitudes that lead to the trustworthiness and mutuality that bring creativity, and allow us to spot quickly those that lead us into fear and conflict.

Creative shortfall

To increase our creative quotient we must become more adaptable, flexible in our response to differences. The rigidities, harshness and harrowing discord that we see throughout society will continue to bring endless conflict. Grappling with our own issues will be a first and vital step in making positive change. Shortcomings in our growth needs often show up as difficulty with difference. Without a steady or sturdy self we may doubt our creativity, fear unduly that our needs will be overlooked and encounter difference with an 'us and them' mentality. Any of these can threaten creative flow because they raise primal fear of losing out in either integrity or resources.

Back to the 3 Essentials

Promoting all three essentials is by and large the master task when aiming to release creativity and ease conflict. There is nothing sadder, or perhaps more dangerous, than harrowing, compound and repetitive conflict. As we encounter a more diverse world we meet and interact with complexity, so it is vital that we become creative players.

In reality, we know that healing is a challenge for all of us; the world in which we live has so much inequality that making a start on promoting creativity is of great importance. Healing is a growth task and that is exactly what we each need to do so that we can begin to play our part in moving from conflict to creativity. Developing all three essentials may require shifts in our outlook. It most certainly will ask for personal adaptability, perseverance and commitment over time, so that the rudiments of a creative way of living can take root. For instance, we may not yet see that creativity is core in each of us, so change in our thinking will be needed. We may not have an adequate baseline in the 5 *Enablers*, so rebalancing may be called for. We may not respect differences. Whatever our personal challenge, we can move forward as soon as we choose to make a change.

When we tailor these changes we will be more successful in staying creative. Easing conflict will be more natural to us.

One by one, step by step, before we know it we will make positive inroads to the essentials. The ideas set out in the next chapters will take us through the terrain. They will provide landmarks that can help us chart a deeper awareness of what it will take to reclaim our creativity.

Part Two will focus on our ability to choose either creativity or conflict. Over the next chapters we will revisit the 3 *Essentials*, this time with a view to making changes that will empower our creative flow. But, first, we must make a choice. For now, let us see how we can make that choice an informed one.

PART TWO

CHOOSING CREATIVITY

CHAPTER 5
CONFLICT OR CREATIVITY –
CAN WE CHOOSE?

Not surprisingly, when it came to writing this book the two words 'creativity' and 'conflict' required unravelling. What helps or hinders when it comes to being creative amid the inevitable conflicts that turn up in all of our lives? Awareness of what either choice really means goes hand-in-hand with making mindful decisions in our negotiations.

At the beginning of this book I said that conflict and creativity are common modes for most of us. We all have experiences where we stay creative, generating trust and upbeat loving emotions, and others where we tip into the conflicts that lead us into negative spirals that eclipse trust. Mostly, however, we are not too bothered to analyse how or why this happens. We may pass it off as good or bad luck. Yet, to become artful in easing conflict we must first do a little untangling of the challenges we face in both creativity and conflict.

Approaching life in a creative spirit will ask us to be more conscious about how we actually *can* ease conflict when we understand the deeper issues that surround it. When we can view the challenge of problems through a more creative lens, we will see that there is always a choice. Knowing more about how we go about making this choice can transform the way we live. My sense is that, more often than not, when we learn more about how both creativity and conflict operate, we will choose to be creative rather than conflictual.

Creativity and conflict

The choice to stay creative is made easier as we learn how to empower our creativity; when we put our insight and know-how into practice. There is a saying that creativity is the 'child of opposites'. Creativity is parented from a mingling of differences. Success lies in being collaborative. Being aware of what makes us creative, and how, given the complexity of life, we can all too readily get mired in conflict, will help us to make a more mindful choice.

As we learn how best to support, encourage and use our innate creativity, we develop a deep sense that escalating conflict is a terrible waste. Yet, to make our choice will involve knowing a little more. Let's begin with the choice to be creative.

Choice 1 - *Creativity*

Sustainable creativity will allow us to expand, innovate and empower one another in ongoing cycles. It is the essence that guides people to care for each other, to play together and to value individual expressiveness. In aiming to live creatively, we tap into the potential that lets us co-create life afresh on a daily basis.

Creative empowerment encourages climates of trust. In our creativity we make families and friendships. We make remedies, solutions, adaptations and services for the problems we meet in our lives. We also make the material stuff for life, the homes we live in, the buildings, the bridges, the parks, the artefacts and services. Creativity in its minutiae may translate into making dinner, telling stories, doing homework, making a sale, trips out, chats in the canteen, doing our job, giving a hand, finding an answer to problems and challenges - whatever. Together, we make our lives and pattern it in our own unique way. As we do so, we are also making new tasks, questions and challenges that must be factored into the nuances of living.

Choice 2 - *Conflict*

With conflict we choose, albeit unconsciously, to engage in an approach that relies on dominance and competition rather than personal empowerment. Within this climate we tend towards a win-lose strategy that fuels opposition and thus breeds excessive fear of losing out. This divides people and disregards the fact that civilized survival favours co-operation.

When we are in conflict, our problem solving takes on a quality of fragmentation, force and power srruggle.

Although competition arises naturally, where an 'all or nothing' - 'have or have not'- approach is promoted, it misses the point of creativity. The spirit of creativity is that there is enough to go around. Peace and prosperity is possible. Few of us take seriously enough the fact that, as organic interconnected beings, we constantly cross-fertilize with one another. While this offers us the gift of relationships that make friendship, love and progress a reality, the flip-side of this connectedness means tensions also get transmitted easily.

When mismatch and tension escalates we may start to feel threatened and fearful. Tensions arise acutely when we go into opposition with one another, either for resources or integrity needs. Opposition fuels conflict and affects each of us, because, as humans, we are porous - our sensory system is constantly sussing our environment. In fear it is only a short hop to projecting all that is perceived as 'bad' on 'them' and all that is seen as 'good' on 'us.' Adoption of 'either / or' thinking will take us into polarities with people and ideas, and can, when severe, create trouble and rigidity. With 'us or them' and 'this or that' thinking we limit possibility, break trust and deaden our creativity.

Acceptance of conflict *and* creativity

Naturally all of us have times when our experience of fear and trust are out of kilter. Loss is an organic part of life, yet our collective human flaws have long histories that, in turn, make for cumulative trauma, producing less than perfect outcomes at times.

Duality is part of our existence, with life and death, day and night, hot and cold and so on. In an authentic life, trust and fear are twins that we bring consciously or unconsciously to most encounters. To live is to have a seasoned relationship with both. To live is to travel territory where differing resources, views and experiences all interplay. We are constantly making choices in the company of both trust and fear as we go about our daily lives. Fear gives us discernment, steps us back, while trust puts us into forward movement. Fear interrupts trust and limits our ability to be creative. In a very general way it will tug at the two great life imperatives popularised by Freud - the imperative to love and the imperative to work. Our fear of losing out gets us into fights, and obscures the reality that we are part of an organic system that depends on inter-dependence.

Trust and creativity

Trustworthiness can connect, humanize and build concern for one another. In trust of others we engage and are engaging. To treat ourselves and others well, to value the spectrum of human needs, is what ultimately helps build trust.

In trust of self we can stand alone to reflect, without losing our capacity to connect in genuine ways. In trusting the good in others we can begin to affirm it. Trust is a 'two-way street' and keeping the aspiration of trust -building alive is an important factor in living creatively. Trust-building will help shape behaviours that, in turn, can 'up' the trust quotient in all of us.

Relating with awareness

Individuals engaged in making meaningful connections with each other is really what positive relationship aims for. Because the inter-connections that build trust can spread out from families across space, time and cultures, it is important to give proper attention to the details that will coax trust. In her book, *The Dance of Connection*, Harriet Lerner says:

"... the thread that unites my work both as an author and as a psychotherapist is my desire to help people speak wisely and well, sometimes about the most difficult subjects. This includes asking questions, getting points across, clarifying desires, beliefs, values, and limits." She also tells the story of two little ones playing together in a sandbox; a fight breaks out and one runs off, saying: "I hate you." Then, in no time at all, they are back playing together as if nothing had happened. An adult nearby comments in admiration: "How do children do that?"

The other replies: "It is simple. They chose happiness over righteousness."

Of course, at our core the child in all of us would rather play than fight. Choosing to be creative asks us to get past our ups and downs, to learn to grieve our losses and trust in the renewal of life that happens around us. To be a player, to live creatively, asks that we do not wallow in the wound but dust ourselves off and start over. Building the trust that releases creativity will always involve 'self' in relationship with others. To be a player, to get past difficulty and to start over in ways that will build trust, is a daily challenge. It is in essence one that must be broken down into the small, regular, renewable steps that let us become creative in sustainable cycles throughout our life.

Within the following chapters of part 2 we will revisit all *three essentials*. We will learn how we can reclaim our creativity by bringing a more conscious focus to all three aspects.

CHAPTER 6
Empowering creative awareness

It's not rocket science

Life truly is one large learning laboratory; because it is, we can manage our change process in the ordinary day-to-day flow. When we have more awareness about the essentials needed for success we can be more circumspect in our choices. It doesn't take rocket science to be true to our human creativity, yet why is it that we have such harsh and cruel contrasts in the treatment of people? Why is the gap between rich and poor so wide? Why are models of competition and exclusiveness so prevalent? Why are there high levels of depression, sickness and poverty around the world? Why is war still legitimate? What needs are going unmet, what challenges are we avoiding, what opportunities are we losing out on? Can we do better?

Chronic loss

The unconscious repeating of conflict patterns is evident in every sphere of life. We see habitual conflict within and between people within families and communities everywhere. The loss we suffer collectively on being disconnected from our creativity is staggering. There is massive untapped talent latent in each of us just waiting to be activated. Writer Denis Potter, talking about a pen that he had lost and describing the longing that goes with loss, said: ... *oh the pen-ness of that pen and the lost-ness of that loss...* Of course, the metaphor of losing his pen is an allegory for what really would be a loss of a vital part of him, i.e. his self-expression. When we lose touch with parts of our self, a blockage of energy can easily take place. And when this happens, pressures mount and symptoms of stress and tension might not be far behind. Neglect and wastage of creative energy can also be pervasive and insidious. Because of this we often overlook warning signs of blockage. We all get sucked in to the negative; getting out of it is the art of being creative. Beautifully captured in the following lines of poetry from David Whyte's *The Heart Aroused*: "It's the world's sore crime that its babes grow dull." It is indeed a reality that growing up tempers enthusiasm and sharpens our critical edge. Yet so much creative enthusiasm is muzzled so soon, that often those who are apparently well off seem unhappy. Recently, a tongue-in-cheek term has come into circulation - 'middlescence.' Coined by Robert Morison, Tamara Erickson and Ken Dychtwald, authors of *Workforce Crisis,* it describes behaviour associated with many long-term middle-aged employees who often present as unhappy and stagnating in their current jobs. In fact, many organizations disregard the primal needs of people and withhold needs, consciously or unconsciously. Where unhappy, bored workers congregate we can hazard a guess that some experiential need is going unmet and creating a roadblock to healthy creative potency. Consciousness of this can take the 'middlescent' out of the doldrums and into creative change.

Lifelong learning models

Even if we feel our creativity is below par, change is always possible and modern psychology now supports the idea that we can tap into new experiences at any time, so a lifelong learning model has replaced old deterministic thinking.

The discovery of our capacity to rework previously arrested developmental tasks was pioneered by psychologist Erik Erickson. He strongly advocates that it is possible to re-do our key developmental tasks throughout our lives. I find the concept that we are always capable of new beginnings very hopeful, as it moves us away from the notion of fixed determinism. It is well accepted that people can change as soon as they make the decision to. Novelist George Eliot advised that it's never too late to be who we are. So many people benefit from an approach that lets them rediscover new facets of their core self and make the changes necessary to give expression to it.

Showing up

Happily, there are now well recognized resources that shape and grow creative awareness in people, and there are plenty of role models and enablers available to help learn and ground these resources. Because we are alive, shaping and reshaping of attitude can be achieved. 'Self' is not one constant thing; it evolves and grows - it gathers momentum, blooms and dies back in phases and cycles right through our lives.

A good time to start

There has never been a better time to access and enable our individual creativity. The huge expansion in the field of personal growth potential is a direct response to people's need to be true to their best self. As people, we actually yearn to own and use our unique creative sap and savvy because most of us are weary of attitudes that lead to war, wastage and wanton living. The desire for personal transformation is surfacing around the globe.

Underpinning this urge is a deep instinctual need to shape and take ownership of our own lives.

At every turn opportunities exist to assist people to change the script that limits their true potential. The slogan 'what we can conceive, we can achieve' is used by attitudinal motivators in all walks of life. This life-long learning approach expands us. It keeps us flexible and adaptive. It matters very little where we start as long as we engage wholeheartedly. The feel good factor that flows from new learning is both energising and contagious.

Making changes

We change and grow through new learning and a change of heart. We get to this through new ideas, play and practice. Through healthy risk we can experiment and make changes. In essence, we learn and change by envisioning something better and doing what it takes to make it happen. When we see clearly what helps us develop a creative attitude we can get it in focus and, little by little, it becomes part of us. As we encounter success at being creative our more destructive tendencies and hindering habits start to lose their sway. They fall away and shrink from lack of use.

Getting past our weaknesses

Psychologist Robert A. Johnson suggests that the solution to woundedness involves individuals brave enough to take the problem personally. This, he says, is the new heroism. It resonates well with those who believe that world affairs can change one person at a time.

Getting past obstacles that block the drawing out of innate creativity will go better with some supportive guidelines. When challenges come to call we may give up too quickly, and yet we so do not have to. With some reference points we can be encouraged to persevere. The rewards begin as we begin. "The sorrow lies in how we refuse to begin the road" - another extract from David Whyte – is a line that speaks volumes.

Imperfect legacy

Even in the affluence of modern western society, our generation and our parents' generation have lived with the persistent shadow of war. Images of war and its casualties have become the norm, even for those of us with no direct experience of war. Life can be fraught for both parents and children, so the need for working and reworking the experiences that shape our attitudes is relevant for all of us. Getting to maturity, like all dynamic living processes, has growth challenges.

Indeed, massive shortfalls in the experiences needed for creative development can happen even in the most normal of childhoods. Tasks of meeting needs can go astray if the parents' ability and home circumstances fall short. It's not hard to imagine how difficult it is for overburdened parents. Perhaps they are touched by death or trauma. Such overwhelming circumstances can compromise parents and children alike.

Or maybe there is no time for children - too much work or play. Perhaps addiction sets in, putting the family system into chaos. Perhaps there is no awareness of development tasks; parents themselves may have received poor care. Or maybe parents are still trying to achieve their own unmet needs and are not coping well with adult life - they may be depressed or uninterested. Yet again maybe the political climate has made it *impossible* for parents to meet needs. Poor childcare and the high cost of living create gaps that can be impossible to close.

Yes, as we are all human and imperfect, in one way or another, we are subject to life's wounding. There is no perfect situation. Shortfalls occur. We see evidence around us every day that some individuals get a higher quota of support than others. Yet there are shortfalls that are relentless, outrageous and appalling. I can hardly overstress that threats to primal needs set in train major problems that have far-reaching consequences. They will trigger fear and have our hackles rise. Trust is eroded when forms of abuse and neglect are perpetuated. Patterns can cross generations in dangerously unconscious ways.

Taking it personally: the new heroism

Written in stone on a temple in Greece is the advice *Know Thyself!* I fancy this old maxim was distilled with great care and precision by the early philosophers who wanted to let us know that, above all else, this must be honoured. So the notion of knowing oneself is not newfangled or New Age; it comes up again and again in each generation to be adapted and grounded in our own time and place. While it seems like an obvious call, in reality many of the experiences we have in families, schools and communities lead us unconsciously to develop habits that steer us away from core selfhood, creative awareness and empowerment. If we find ourselves trapped in a life where others impose and manipulate our choices, we will lose out. If we cannot connect with our true self and take the rough with the smooth, we cannot integrate and become whole. Relationships may fail, opportunity may be missed. Where this happens, a phoney or wounded self can easily become a disempowered self. If we settle into patterns that disconnect us from our real self we may only thread the surfaces of our lives. When this happens we risk drifting reactively through life, never harnessing or being invigorated by our true personal strengths. Psychologist Carl Rodgers, whose life work centred on helping people to become the person they truly are, believed that coming into your own autonomous power could be termed the 'quiet revolution.'

The personal revolution

Ideally, childhood is the time to tutor and unfold creativity - so that we are helped on a course that can recognise and draw out our strengths and talents. Where this happens, we become conditioned for renewable cycles of creativity for the whole of our lifespan. When surfaces of our lives are aligned with the deeper connection that fuels and recharges our passion for living, we are energised quite naturally. 'Ideally,' however, is an important word here because even the best of child-hoods, as already said, may leave a need to rework some development tasks. Reworking our developmental needs will take us into a deeper encounter with our truest self.

If we miss out on this connection, we may habitually wear masks rather than show our real face. Living from surfaces only, we may encourage homogenising and compulsive sanitizing. In not knowing our full self we may tend to create polarities and cut-offs - to edit and dismiss the bits we do not like. Old hurts and poor thought patterns can hold us prisoner and, although familiar, they might not be good for us or for others. When we can unfold a more rounded, resilient and compassionate self, the going gets easier.

Negativity flooding our consciousness blocks our creativity. Shallow and surface living ultimately comes across as less real. Maybe the expression 'lacking soul' speaks to the absence of connection with core being.

The good news is that, when the habits that hold us back get sorted, the urge to be in flow and in balance with the best in ourselves and others is what comes most easily. Yet, while it does not take rocket science to grow and develop a creative attitude, it does take focused attention and a willingness to give the time and space to basic changes that bring it about. Paradoxically, in trying to avoid pain, people can keep meeting it by unconsciously repeating patterns. Some go on to repeat cycles of neglect and abuse in an unconscious way because they have not been able to face their inner pain, a first necessary step for their own healing. D. H. Lawrence suggested that "consciousness is the new aristocracy." Certainly, we have the know-how and resources to make major positive changes in the world, but first we must become conscious of how we can empower our own creativity. As soon as we do begin to bring our attention towards change, we start the process of living and stop denying, blocking or truncating our creative potential. We do it for ourselves first, but we do it for others too, because a creative charge in ourselves shines out to others, just as stagnation tempers and dulls. It is a given that we are each unique and have different levels of need, different gifts and challenges. This is important to grasp.

Without a 'depth charge' that connects us with our true self we can find it hard to connect with others in anything but superficial ways. When we know ourselves, we begin to value genuineness and personal empowerment so dearly that a pastiche version of 'self' feels awkward and wasteful.

Creativity-privilege and task

As we begin to commit ourselves to living from our creative core life throws up synchronicities together with challenges. These change and shape our attitudes as we go about the minutiae of daily life. The experiences of both *via positiva and via negativa* will each produce gradual, helpful shifts in our process of change.

Some aspects of becoming creative will ask us to harden up; to use our heads. A little like the hot house flowers, some of our past experiences may only have prepared us for a challenge-free life; others may need a softening as our approach to life does not have to be harsh or hard.

With a creative attitude we are fully engaged in unfurling and shaping our deepest and truest self. Life in all its varying phases and stages can be resourced and managed from this abundant wellspring. When we have a creative attitude we can encourage interplay, collaboration, productivity and innovation. With such an attitude we can each play our part and make progress in the full spectrum of global issues.

Because creativity gives variety, interest and meaning to the complexity of life, we will learn to accept and celebrate life in all its hues.

People power

Help may show up in unexpected places and relationships. It may be something generous that requires unselfish commitment. It may be a tangible gift or a kind and honest challenge. It may be a loss, a shortfall that spurs our creative path-finding. Help may come from a family member, a trusted friend, a professional or a chance encounter. In the movement of life, when we can stay attuned to engaging creativity, the connections we need generally turn up. Conversations with a variety of people can help us clarify and gain a wider perspective.

Indeed, thanks are always due to a myriad of inputs when we foster a creative spirit. What goes around, comes around. Because we are by nature relational, we can really only come to know ourselves fully in the narratives of relationship. No amount of therapy will replace the ongoing need for a variety of friendships and ordinary day-to-day relationships that make up life.

The healing task

The healing task is always a growth task. To grow will ask for change. It will ask that we grieve our losses, soothe our hurts and bring better balances to our lives.

Writing recently in the *Financial Times,* Rupert Merson offered words of wisdom on approaching the need for new growth in business. He might well have been talking about the new growth required in the healing process when he gave this sound advice:

"Growth in business is a series of crises punctuated by periods of smoother evolution. Every time you get one of those chunky changes you are going to precipitate a crisis. You need to recognise that those periods of crises are not unique to yourself and others have passed through them successfully."

The healing evolution, too, can be challenging and can seem for some of us an added burden in our day-to-day working lives, yet as we gradually gain valuable know-how we learn to shed the burdens that block us and begin to enjoy the lightness of a creative approach.

Uncovering our strength

Making a start at anything usually involves caring enough to begin and to commit. When we value a creative attitude and when we can give energy to developing it, over time, it takes hold in our lives and radiates on to all that surrounds us. Defensive behaviours can become so entrenched that they then cease to be protective and become a problem in, and of, themselves. These defences that were intended to protect can actually create walls and obstacles to relationship in every sphere of our life. The trouble with keeping painful memories and feelings at bay is that we are also keeping our potential at bay. If we cannot look at our weakness, we block the flow of our real strength.

Depth charging

Blockages can obscure awareness of the creative source available to us. Yet, with a clear connection to our core creative center we can experience our authentic power. As we experience this, we believe in our own worth and in the worth of others, and can relish each other's rich and varied strands. If we understand and buy into the awareness that, as people, we are inter-connected and innately creative, we will, as night follows day, ease our conflicts.

As adults, the choice of attitude then is ours to make.

When we have experiences that encourage our creative capacity we get softer, stronger and more compassionate; we can then relate to ourselves and others in a more truthful and genuine way. This change of approach can transform the way we deal with conflict.

As we live creatively, we get to value it as real, worthwhile and essential. When we trust and commit ourselves to this most basic capacity, it becomes constant, we then begin to fuel a vital and vibrant way of life. With creativity all of us can express our multifaceted natures again and again in each season of our lives. Rising to the challenge will ask us to become seasoned in embracing life in its fullness. Nobody else can do it for us.

Hand-in-hand with valuable know-how

Professional help can make a vital contribution when embarking on healing changes. Before we mature we are needy in ways that help pull the experiences we need to us. As we move to re-enable creativity we have to approach it in a more mindful way. The role of any therapeutic input is to empower the individual. Facilitation with a trusted individual is a great support; over time, it can help initiate us into the *modus vivendi* of healthy relating. The task in hand will involve identifying outworn habits that hold us back from our creativity, the process of change will be eased with skilled support.

Our creative unfurling will go more smoothly when we have an understanding of what helps and what hinders. There may be skins to shed; old worn out defences that once seemed protective may be impeding our creative unfurling. Sometimes, like the lobster, we must shed a shell in order to grow; like the lobster we may have hardened armour that needs to go if we want to grow.

Some of us require more assistance, while others progress with fewer inputs - people differ.

Expert help is always welcome, yet our own subjective view is of paramount importance. Remember - because we each have our own unique blueprint that is unfurled with a mixture of support and challenge, it cannot be over-emphasised that empowering autonomy, self-reliance and interdependence is a central ethic when we work to facilitate creativity.

Today's world offers an abundance of supports that bring specialized and competent guidance as we move into making changes. There are books that offer clarity, encouragement and guidelines. There are therapeutic supports that come in all shapes ready to help. Websites, too, have speeded up access to information. The interventions and inputs of a skilled helper, together with the resources around us, can be the makings of our planned changes. We can avail ourselves of others' experiences by networking and learning from their practice wisdom. So, whether in tandem with therapeutic know-how or within our personal network, or both, we can, once we decide to, begin making the changes that help ease conflict and promote creativity.

Through a mixture of care and challenge, each of us can get to maturity. Through being helped to be self-aware we access the creative core available to us. Thomas Moore in his book, *Care of the Soul*, takes up this concept when he says: "In offering acceptance to the genuine unfolding self we set up the love of self that paradoxically we need before we can maturely love another." Self-care, then, can be viewed as the first step in caring for others. Letting go of baggage and unleashing our potential will take some commitment, effort and wisdom. In the next chapter we re-visit the *5 Enablers* and we see how better balances in these will be a central task in accessing our creativity.

CHAPTER 7
Empowering the enablers

Better balances

Balance is a key to health. It is however, not a fixed state. We make constant shifts in order to maintain it. Balance is kept by staying flexible, by adapting to changes and circumstances as they arise. Healthy balance is a dance of equilibrium. Yes, the inner impetus towards wholeness is always trying to rectify, to balance. It will aim in any way it can, adaptively or maladaptively.

So it follows that, when we want to ease conflict, we may need to understand a little more about how balances operate in our own lives. Getting better balances in the *5 Enablers* will be important because, drawing out our innate creativity in a sustainable way, as we have seen, really does depend on each of us having an optimal level in these legitimate and primary needs. Habit patterns that flow from shortfall or excess can become hardened, fixed and disenabling of creative development. Such patterns are passed on, encoded and engrained in society. Improving conditions of shortfall and excess in the social realm engages many institutions and service providers. Yet individually, unconscious patterns can be tenacious. Because improving balances in these needs can take time, we know that change will take patience. Poor habits are not given up all at once - we have to make gradual shifts over time.

Deficits create the conditions of fear and counter-fear; they play out in extremes that, should they become a way of life, can be harmful for us and others. Fear for our primal needs makes us defensive, and can, at the extreme, get us stuck in rigidities and polarities. Fixed, fear-based thinking puts us out of balance.

When fear patterns last a long time they become hardened habits that will make us inflexible. Such patterns in extreme tip us into ruts of under or overdevelopment in our human needs index. While many people do achieve aspects of each of the *5 Enabler* needs at optimal levels, however underdeveloped and overdeveloped aspects are part of everyone's life at some time or other. To become aware of this is to begin our path to enabling creative empowerment for all of us. When we live with unmet developmental needs, we can go through our lives unconsciously seeking to rectify imbalances. Becoming conscious is what really directs the change.

Consciousness is key

Many people never get to mature fully because, while change is a certainty, progress is not; many of us live with no broad insight about how to empower our creative potential. When we are unaware we can often repeat the past unconsciously. It is like having an underground volcano of old wounds and grudges bubbling with intensity, all belonging to the past but erupting and seeping through to the present. Little is resolved if we refuse to grow in self-awareness.

To take responsibility, to meet our needs is, in essence, to start making the world a better place. As we get the measure of it we can pass it on. In particular, we need awareness of the essentially creative nature that is unleashed when needs are met. When we understand how needs work, we can know ourselves better and appreciate that creativity is at our fingertips in every situation - ours for the choosing. We don't have to wait another minute to begin.

Becoming more aware of our own creative nature is the most empowering and rewarding decision we can make. New levels of awareness will transform how we deal with conflicts. The reward of reworking our needs is that it connects us to our creative power. It moves us beyond the emotional fallout, beyond the pain that comes from loss and regret.

First things first

Naturally, all of us have times when we experience being off-centre; we lack balance - the mark of maturity is to be able to recognise it. It is only when we get stuck in persistent and unconscious habits of excess and shortfall that patterns harden and polarities get us into trouble. Below we can see again at a glance (details at chapter two and three), what optimal levels in the 5 *Enablers* can bring about:

Level 1 - Optimal *Survival Needs*
Give and receive in balance = equitable share

Level 2 - Optimal *Security Needs*
Risk and protection in balance = healthy limits

Level 3 - Optimal *Belonging Needs*
Connection and separation in balance = inter-relationship

Level 4 - Optimal *Esteem Needs*
Self-worth and humility in balance = intrinsic worth

Level 5 - Optimal *Capability Needs*
Inner aptitude and outer skill in balance = authentic expression

Yet before we can agree to work for better balances, we need to know that imbalances in the 5 *Enablers* do cause problems. We need to know, too, how imbalance plays out. Doing an audit and taking seriously our shortcomings or excesses, we can begin to process the behaviours, thoughts or emotional changes we need to make. Successful balancing of the *5 Enablers* will transform how we manage conflict and will help us live with a truly creative spirit.

Making a start

Exploring starts by taking a close look at how needs are working in our lives. For example, in dealing with the *5 Enablers,* any one area may be feeling the effects of an imbalance. Each need imbalance will play out in its own way in keeping with personality and situation. Each need missed out on, when it reaches tipping point, leads us to adopt a compensatory stance. Over time when left unconscious they will affect our creative spirit. Working to maintain balance is therefore well worth aiming for.

Balancing the enablers

In the circles below, we will see how each one of the *5 Enablers* has an optimal balance, yet each can tilt away from the *optimal* into an imbalance. Extreme in either direction can cause us trouble. We lose out when we stay in extremes. Over time we can develop thoughts, behaviours and feelings that hold us back from our creative best. Being stuck in either lack or excess can be damaging. We now know that without an ability to balance we cannot adapt, so we lose the flexibility to achieve creative solutions. However, there is no fixed perfection; instead, the consciousness that lets us check in, stay flexible and adapt is what determines our creative success. And, yes, we all have our own areas that require a graceful tempering. Given this, when we know where and how we are held back from being creative, we can start to rebalance as the need dictates. This will inevitably ease the stress and strain that trigger fear and lead to a spectrum of conflictual responses.

Let's begin with the first need, survival.

Enabler 1. *Survival*

When fear operates at this level we might be feeling stuck with an unconscious sense of fear for our basic survival needs, and when that fear reaches a critical level, it puts us out of balance; we find ourselves moving away from an optimal level into an extreme.

Caring for the basics of shelter, food and warmth lays down our ability to be kind. Balanced nurture humanises us. It is found in family kinship and, indeed, in the friendships of our communities. Harshness, starvation and helplessness are often the legacy of poor nurture. Learning to share fairly is brought about as we have the experience of it; giving and receiving can hardly be activated if we have no experience of it. Effects of poor nurture can last a lifetime and create poverty mentalities for successive generations. Wastage from greed and stockpiling creates problems too, particularly in that it can cause stagnation and ruin trust in creative cycles of filling and emptying, giving and receiving. There is great imbalance in resource distribution in our world today. We have not yet developed a mass consciousness that can grasp the fact that starvation and stockpiling are connected. Wounds in this area show up in our ability to share fairly. For instance, when out of balance it can affect our ability for give and take; we find it hard to be generous or to trust that we have a right to receive.

Level 1 - Optimal *Survival Needs*

Give and receive in balance = Equitable share

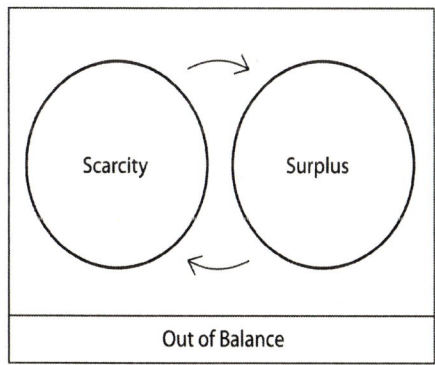 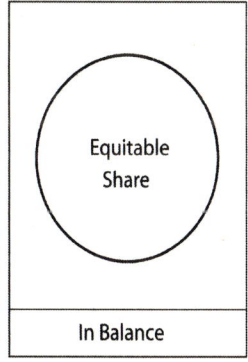

Imbalance triggers conflict

An imbalance in terms of our survival needs will also trigger the destructive conflict responses that bind us into scarcity and overgrasping cycles. Withholding from ourselves and others creates patterns of meanness that narrow our spirits and encourage poverty. The trouble comes in the way that such thinking permeates our ability to negotiate fair play. The management of resources, whether in the business or domestic world, can be traced to wounds both cultural and personal at this first survival level. At worst, wounds can play havoc, creating the cycles of scarcity and greed that inform the way we live. At best, these wounds, when they show up and are recognised, will offer an imperative for learning a new approach that creates better balances. Balance in this area paves the way for a willingness to exchange. The very first requirement of creativity is the capacity to share.

Sharing - achieving balance

Sharing is therefore fundamental to creativity. Balancing, giving and receiving is the foundation stone on which easing conflict is built.

One way or another survival issues that are not surfaced and healed can prevent us learning a more graceful approach to give and take. Whatever realm of life we operate in, if we have not healed our basic nurture needs we may find our attitude tipped out of balance towards, on one hand, shortfall and, on the other, surplus. Both are traps. At the scarcity end of the spectrum we are doomed to live in misery. When we fear at this level - the basics - our pattern will tip us into scarcity; we then fear that there will never be enough. We may sell ourselves short; we may not expect enough; we may internalise scarcity and create a self-fulfilling prophecy of scarcity - both for ourselves and others.

In this frame of mind creativity cannot thrive. We cannot be receptive when we are stuck in a scarcity trap. The very thing that allows us to receive is blocked by the negative thinking of scarcity. On the opposite side, we become greedy and enough is never enough – the wastage of stockpiling or surplus become a norm. We cannot be generative when we hold too tight.

We are unable to give so we block the flow of energy. Either extreme will sabotage the creative. Balancing and bridging these two extremes is an ongoing challenge and largely a matter of learning to be conscious of good balances. Exchange of energy and passing on human nurture is the most fundamental life skill and, indeed, the most noble.

Enabler 2. *Security*

The sheer fact of being alive and having choices asks us to grapple with risk. Everything from excitement to extreme fear may come up in the multiple life choices and challenges we make daily. If we have good inner radar we know when to move forward to take a risk, and when to stand back and critique wisely. In the course of an ordinary day people choose to meet some challenges while shying away from others. To be protective will ask us to close off - to be more circumspect, more measured in our approach. Depending on the circumstances, we can choose. We can run into difficulty in our negotiations as we will see later if we are overly open where it might be better to remain more clos*ed - and vice versa,* where we are overly closed when we should remain open. The way we respond to challenges often tells us a lot about how we are operating at this second level need.

Level 2 - Optimal *Security Needs*
Risk and protection in balance = Healthy Limits

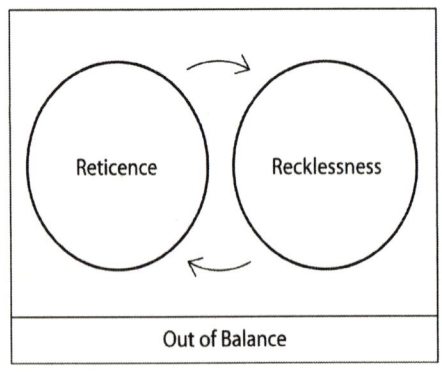
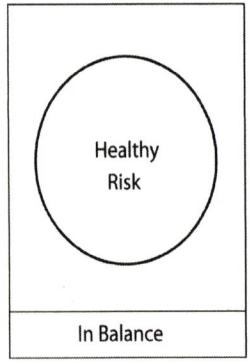

Imbalance triggers conflict

Being out of balance in either limits our creative flow. On the one hand, without the ability to risk we become timid and may not face or engage with challenge, so depriving ourselves of the explorations that build success. On the other hand, we may lunge forward recklessly, unaware of real dangers. Either can tip and sabotage a sustainable creative process. When we overly resist taking a chance, or take dangerous risks, sustainable creativity may go astray. We may miss opportunities because we get stuck in ruts or destroy progress by being reckless.

Deep-rooted imbalances in this area create insecurities that, until healed and integrated, can stymie our creative explorations and cause difficulties.

Developmentally, the process of learning to explore and discover on our own initiative begins early in life and is affected by the level of safety and challenge in the environment in which we find ourselves. Today, getting this subtle balance is a preoccupation for many parents. Overprotection and underprotection can leave room for victim-abuser cycles to thrive. Making the world safer is a concern for caring individuals everywhere. When we feel unsafe we start to build defences, the very thing that closes off new discoveries for possibility in relationships and, consequently, in the possibility for creativity. The challenge at this level involves balancing healthy risk and protection. Without risk one cannot creatively be a player. Exploration, co-operation and cross-fertilizing of our ideas will all be hampered by imbalances in this area. Above all else, healthy risk fuels the creative engines that move us to encounter new ideas, people and places.

Security - achieving balance

Risk-takers tend to have developed stress hardiness; they see failure as part of the eventual process that leads to success.

"Fail again. Fail better" was the advice of the writer-dramatist Samuel Beckett. In this way failure becomes part of success. Discovery asks us to start over and enter experience with freshness, to forgive and to have compassion for what it means to be human in a world full of dangers.

The behaviours that flow from destructive conflict are the kiss of death to the kind of co-operative exploration, encounter and interaction that is vital to our creativity.

Healthy risk asks us to be open, to be flexible in taking a chance and to have a radar that shows where limits are needed. This is mostly a matter of learning to discern and to be resilient. The stress of challenge and chance is part and parcel of risk.

By definition, risk is uncertain and the higher the stakes, the more it calls for preparedness. Risking, exploring, experimenting and playing are all vital to creativity and are dependent on developing safe boundaries. Having a healthy boundary, the ability to be open and to have a capacity to have limits, is vital to relationships. Rigidly closed or overly open boundaries put us out of balance. Adequate safety levels are built experientially in a gradual way. When healthy protection and risk is grounded in us our antennae for safety and danger are activated and we learn healthy risk. Finding a happy medium, where the dignity of risk and protection can co-exist, is becoming a challenge for wider society.

Enabler 3. *Belonging*

How we first experience belonging can affect our participation and involvement later on as we move into wider society. Being part of a family in and of itself is protective - being abandoned or made an outsider clearly presents a danger. Yet, being overly bound to our family group may cause us to lose our individualism. Some families do not allow for differences - sameness and conformity is insisted upon. In others, children are not allowed the comfort of the close ties that help us feel contained and cohesive. So great is a child's need to belong that they may give up their innate drive for autonomy in order to feel closely bonded.

How we make attachments and become separate individuals in our first and early experiences has great impact for us. This essential two-step 'dance' enables us to hold on and let go appropriately - to connect with others and to be a separate individual also. This is a universal need and getting balance is what helps us inter-relate in healthy ways.

Level 3 - Optimal *Belonging Needs*

Connection and separation in balance = inter-relationship

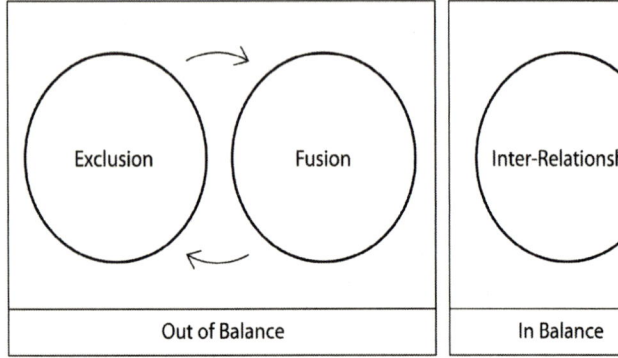

Out of Balance	In Balance

Imbalance triggers conflict

Out of balance at one extreme, we may have had a feeling that we are not part of a family; we feel excluded, have the experience of truncated or fragmented attachment. A cold, clinical and distant climate may have existed where we felt relations were non-engaging or on a purely functional basis. A little like a benevolent institution where warm connection and interest in us was not available. The natural childhood need to merge and feel a part of the family - the experience of oneness in the family - was refused us. Family therapists sometimes call this an experience of being 'disengaged.' Here a feeling of exclusion dominates. Where our experience of connection has perhaps left us with a feeling of fusion, we lean to the enmeshed. Family therapists use this term when referring to the experience of being part of a great amorphous mass, where individuality is not only discouraged but exhibiting difference can spell abandonment, or is met with sanction. Often such patterns develop from fear, and a drive to over-protect. They can be a misguided *good* intention to protect group coherence. In extreme such a pattern is troublesome because it prevents the healthy individuation that is formed in separateness and is a normal passage of growing up.

Wounds in our experience of belonging can show up in either direction and can make for tendencies towards overplay or underplay in terms of interrelating. These are often the things that show up in our conflicts. Healthy connection and healthy distancing does not take place in either extreme. Loss in this area can affect our ability to take our space as an individual, to feel that we are connected and have boundaries that can *help us* feel a sense of self.

Conflict sets in where people feel excluded or at risk of being taken over.

Interrelating - achieving balance

Balancing connection and separateness is central to relating. It is an ongoing interplay with self and other. *We can make it together*, be team players. In reality there is nothing else. Imbalances in this area can stop us from being creative. Not only is no man an island but connectivity is what moves energy to and fro, making and shaping our lives. Later we will come back to this subject when we look at the dynamics of fairness in negotiation.

Enabler 4. *Esteem*

The need to be esteemed arises in every child. A healthy need to be seen, respected and have loving relationships is normal. To be young, childlike and egocentric, while enjoying stable, consistent parenting that mirrors, models and affirms the best in us, is an ideal. There is a real crisis in the world at present around meeting core, person-centred needs - commercialism and fast-track living overly focus on image and goal achievement to the detriment of the personal and relational. If we experience being undervalued, it is easy to suffer low *self-esteem* - and with that we are self-depreciating and perhaps self-destructive. We can also be depreciating or destructive of the worth of others.

Wounds in this level are played out in imbalances in self- awareness.

Level 4 - Optimal *Esteem Needs*

Self-worth and humility in balance = Intrinsic Worth

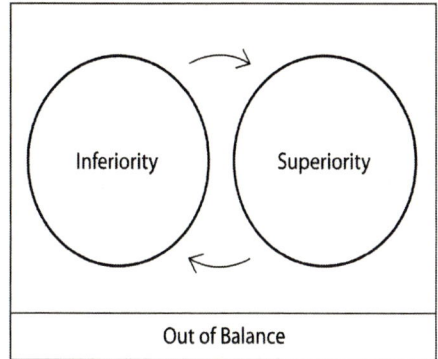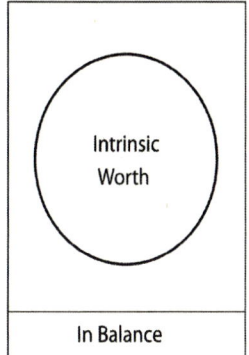

Imbalance triggers conflict

Imbalance at the level of esteem can take the form of inferiority or superiority. These are often at play in conflict tugs-of-war. When wounds play out in inferiority, we are likely to be tipped into a feeling of worthlessness. We may feel de-valued, unworthy, undeserving, and unlovable. When these imbalances are at the opposite extreme, our feelings tend towards aggrandising, self-centeredness, where an illusion of *'better than"* can dominate. Either extreme can lead to behaviours that fuel conflict.

Depreciating oneself or others can lead to disrespect, disregard or degradation. These are often the imbalanced attitudes that trigger massive outbursts of rage in conflict situations where human dignity has been eroded. When we cannot connect with our true self - we lose out. Autonomy, for this reason, can be viewed as the human right that underpins democracy. Many systems and regimes, secular and religious, disregard the individual creativity. This ultimately crushes personal empowerment.

With a person-centred approach, people matter. Each of us has an intrinsic dignity quite apart from how our behaviour might categorize it. We are much more than our behaviour. While behaviour and the conditions that give rise to it can be challenged, outlawed or neutralized, the personal dignity of the person is essential. Ury and Fisher gave us the slogan, 'hard on issues, soft on people.' Where a person-centered approach is operating, our behaviour becomes more ethical and principled. Treating others and ourselves with respect allows for principled, ethical living. It steers away from withholding and power struggle. The natural need to be respected for our own unique self is dearly prized within all of us, whatever level of aptitude we actually have.

People differ, yet respect for our core humanity is an aspiration that never leaves us. All individuals are born with healthy narcissistic needs - the need to be seen and affirmed is a phase in normal childhood development.

Narcissistic wounding comes about when we feel undervalued or worthless. In her book, *The Drama of Being a Child,* psychologist Alice Miller talks about how narcissistic rage frequently occurs in adults. This is a rage with an intensity that belongs to the past and is a response to an unmet healthy need to have one's intrinsic value acknowledged and affirmed.

Not surprisingly, when we have angry feelings of this intensity it will mean difficulty in relationship. When esteem needs are lost out on, the young ego can split off, losing a connection with the core authentic self. This is how one becomes prone to a self-aggrandisement that makes one feel superior, at its opposite takes on a sense of inferiority. As we experience balance in self-esteem, we learn to be more autonomous, more real and, consequently, more honest. These qualities allow a genuine and mutual valuing to take place, one that will enhance the win-win climate for our negotiations. We will return to this later; for now, remember that balancing our self-esteem is central to releasing the creativity that can ultimately bring ease to conflict.

Intrinsic Worth – achieving Balance

Holding the conviction that we humans are part of an immense creative system encourages belief in the dignity of the individual, because ultimately it is how we individuals draw on and contribute to the whole. Respect for this then is the surest way to affirm a creative spirit.

To have esteem is to have feelings of self-worth - to know our inner core being.

To promote self-worth is to value the intrinsic dignity of ourselves and others. When we do, we can be creative. Sustainable creativity requires reverence in the way we approach life. Because it is respect for interconnections, big and small, that help each of us make our own unique contribution. In being creative we begin to experience others and ourselves as the conduits that make progress possible.

A person-centered approach holds that it is desirable for people to develop their inner integrity and not seek to dominate or control others. 'Power over' attitudes inevitably offends our intrinsic right to self-determination.

People are deemed important. Our behaviour is aimed at being humanistic. The behaviours that flow from this approach are essentially ethical and principled. These principles are, of course, the necessary supports to channel sustainable creativity.

This approach is passed on generation after generation. The reverse is also true. Much tyrannical behaviour can be traced back to harsh and cruel childhoods. Valuing people works well and builds our capacity for warmth and love. It is the sad reality that many harsh patterns repeat themselves. To become clear about them, is to learn from them and, ultimately, heal and transform them.

Enabler 5. *Capability*

We become capable by combining our inner aptitude with skill. We cannot express our creativity without both. Each plays a part in making us capable. When we are off balance in this area, creative empowerment will be lacking, expressiveness may be difficult; we may be caught in either under-reach or over-drive and we may find it hard to have the confidence to express ourselves truly.

Level 5 - Optimal *Capability Needs*

Inner aptitude and skill in balance = authentic expression

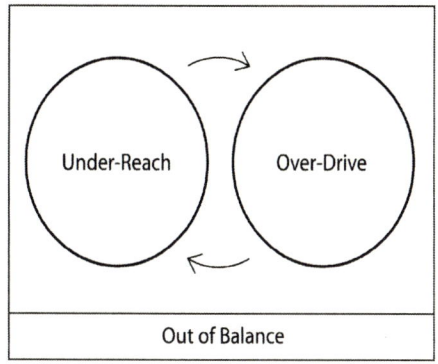
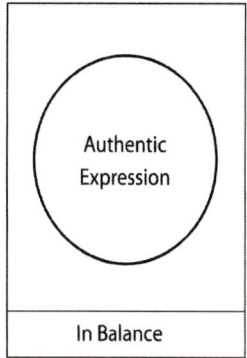

Imbalance triggers conflict

Many conflicts that arise are triggered by lack of empowerment in this area. Shortfalls in our confidence can make us quarrelsome, because most conflict is triggered by fear of powerlessness. Many conflicts are worsened by feelings of disempowerment - when we feel incapable of being fully expressive, we cannot bring our ideas into form. When we play out unconscious patterns of under-reach and over-drive either can cause problems for sustainable creativity.

At one extreme we may present the lack of skill and know-how that leave us feeling stuck. At the other, burn-out may occur from overdrive. Capability needs, as we can see, are interconnected and have their roots in the partnership between our upbringing and training.

Authentic Expression - Achieving Balance

Travelling through life with the spirit of adventure that leads us to make new learning and sustainable creativity our primary focus will mean that we can create in renewing cycles throughout our lives. This is truly what it means to journey creatively. When we learn to bring our ideas from the realm of imagination into form, we can be authentically expressive. We can identify what it is we want to do and set about finding the skill to do it. Significant shortfalls in the area of capability will affect our creativity; we may lack skills and knowledge or self-discipline and fall short of the practice necessary to reach mastery for our creative endeavours. Educational systems can help so much in bringing out the innate talents that will build confidence. To be fair, many educational systems do a great job, yet, as has ever been the case, some individuals lose out by falling through gaps caused by the compound effect of unresolved obstacles at home and at school.

Stressors come up in many guises. Stress will delay or even prevent learning. Early in life, school ethos may be influenced by teachers who themselves are caught in wounds of low empowerment and pseudo-empowerment; they can transmit negativity that will challenge some children to their core. Yet many teachers do a wonderful job; they grapple with children who arrive in school with low esteem and poor containment. Commitment to personal needs enablement is central to children's creative empowerment. For this reason, becoming aware of imbalances and developing the attitudes that promote life-long learning is of crucial importance. Adult education is flourishing and the great news is that, as adults, we have a lot of life experience to draw on, so we can bring more to any of our chosen endeavours.

Review and assess

Those five enabling experiences that we have just covered can be reworked. When we recognize our own imbalances we can begin to ask ourselves about what needs changing? When we learn about how imbalance plays out, we can be more conscious and focused in rebalancing the experiences that we need.

No matter what point we find ourselves at, we can make a start, we can create better balance. Remember there will often be bumps on the road and some difficulties may seem overburdening. Step back, take a break. When we start to feel more balanced in our needs we will feel lighter. As we do, and re-do this, we settle into the essence of our creative nature. In the next chapter, we can approach the 5 *Enablers* with a view to doing a personal audit. In doing so, we can identify the attitudinal and practical changes that will bring about better balances in all five areas.

CHAPTER 8
BALANCING THE ENABLERS

A balancing act

Dr Edward Bach, author of *The Twelve Healers*, suggested that, when we find a tendency in ourselves that is overdeveloped or underdeveloped, we must not overly focus on the problem dimension, rather we can begin to balance simply by putting our attention on cultivating its complementary opposite. Doing this begins, he suggests, to gradually break a habit and bring balance.

Balancing the 5 Enablers

When we bring conscious energy to the issue on hand, with practice, we will meet success. Over time optimal levels evolve and we are saved from getting stuck in extreme polarities. In this way, our troublesome habitual shortcomings and excesses start to be managed. We stay flexible, moving in the rhythms of daily life, balancing needs. It is in this way we learn the art of easing conflict. So we make a start by becoming conscious of where imbalances operate and how they impact. When we become clear and decisive about what changes we want to make, the doing gets easier.

We can begin at our own pace to take on the challenge of auditing and reviewing.

Audit and balance

Personal awareness of how imbalances in the 5 *Enablers* can cause problems is important to healing. To *un-learn* old destructive patterns, we will need to do some form of audit. Good diagnosis is a large part of effective healing - put more plainly, if we don't know where the problem lies we cannot remedy it. It is true to say that when we have lost out development in one or all of the 5 *Enablers* - survival, security, belonging, esteem and capability - we are always consciously or unconsciously seeking to redress these imbalances. This, of course, is as it should be. Seeking consciously it is not a problem because, as we will see later, we can make changes that will re-balance excess or shortfall. When we do, we will move to meet our needs in a more focused and surefooted way. Seeking *unconsciously* to redress the imbalances is the difficult one, because trying to meet needs in this way may result in more 'chance change' than meaningful change.

If we are keen to ease conflict, acceptance of the fact that we all have legitimate needs will be paramount. By doing our part to promote consciousness of these human needs, we will become empowered in a genuine way - we enable ourselves and, in turn, we can enable others too.

To help further awareness about needs, and how to achieve greater balance around them, is our task. Each need lost out on can generate its own debilitating tendency and pattern. Needs we have lost out on in significant ways can create serious patterns of imbalance and sabotage our creativity. To meet this challenge we must become aware of how particular shortfalls and excesses can cause problems. In doing so, we will discover how, by simply questioning, we will begin to bring more awareness.

Often we put off getting better balances because we become stuck in ruts, seeing no way through. We can forget that dynamic humans have vast potential to initiate attitude changes. Attitude change is always the beginning of real practical change. For instance:

Enabler 1 *(Survival) may require a practical and attitudinal shift towards balancing giving and receiving.*

Enabler 2 *(Security) may require a practical and attitudinal shift towards balancing risk and protection.*

Enabler 3 *(Esteem) may require a practical and attitudinal shift towards balancing value and humility.*

Enabler 4 *(Belonging) may require a practical and attitudinal shift towards balancing connection and separation.*

Enabler 5 *(Capability) may require a practical and attitudinal shift towards balancing aptitude and skill.*

Better balances - the start of easing conflict

When we take seriously the impact of imbalances in our own individual life, we can start to make shifts and changes. Re-balancing will ease conflicts big and small. While there is no perfection and life can sometimes throw us off course, we will make mistakes, yet we can find our way back.

In time, we learn that conflict is not the problem, but that our limited ways of responding to it can be. Where optimal balance exists, moving through our conflicts becomes easier.

We can learn to be inclusive and broad when it comes to understanding our own and others' needs. We can become responsible for making changes.

Questioning Exercise

Finding out where our own needs are under or overdeveloped will be a first step. However, if serious deficits exist, you may want, as I have suggested, to have a caring professional support that will coach and mirror progress. We all have some patterns that block us. Taking a chance to make some changes is all it takes to get our creativity back in flow.

Drawing on the aspirations for optimal balance set out in Chapter 7, we can seek to stay centered and make some changes that can pave the way for easing conflict.

We begin by asking are our survival needs being met in a balanced way? Or perhaps it is a security need that is under pressure. Commonly played out is our feeling of belonging; are we having issues with participation? What about our self-esteem - is it being compromised or hurt? Maybe our feeling of competence is less than it needs to be. Whatever the level of imbalance, challenge or threat, a settling can come about when we have insight and commitment to create better balances. Whether one or all of the enablers need attention will be an individual matter. Taking note of imbalances as you notice them will help guide your personal creative revival. Questioning the balances in these experiences that shape and pattern creativity will help.

So to consciously begin to balance our needs, we must ask where we have a lack or an excess. For instance, here are some suggestions of what we might ask when doing a personal inventory;

Level 1 - Optimal *Survival*

Give and receive in balance = equitable share
Enabler 1 (Survival) - Am I experiencing adequacy of nurture - food and warmth - or have I a pattern of depletion operating in my life? How do I act this out? Am I caught in unconscious scarcity or greed traps? Be specific. Write it out

Level 2 - Optimal *Security*

Risk and protection in balance = healthy limits
Enabler 2 (Security) - Am I experiencing personal se-curity or am I operating with a pattern of timidity or recklessness? Are there areas where I need to take some risks or areas where I am being reckless? How would it be more balanced? Be specific. Write it out

Level 3 - Optimal *Belonging*

Connection and separation in balance = inter-relationship
Enabler 3 (Belonging) - Am I experiencing healthy connection and separateness? Is fusion or exclusion an issue? How would it be more balanced? Be spe-cific. Write it out

Level 4 - Optimal *Esteem*

Self-worth and humility in balance = intrinsic worth
Enabler 4 (Esteem) - Am I experiencing personal value and regard or am I trapped in a pattern of feel-ing inferiority or superiority? How would it be more balanced? Be specific. Write it out.

Level 5 - Optimal *Capability*

Inner aptitude and skill in balance = authentic expression
Enabler 5 (Capability) - Have I the skill to bring my ideas into form? Or have I patterns of over-reach and under-reach? How would it be more balanced? Be specific. Write it out.

These questions may help spotlight areas that need your attention. Reflecting on these will pave the way for change.

Inalienable *5 Enabler* experiences

The *5 Enabler* experiences remain the inalienable formative experiences for releasing our creativity. Difficulty at any stage with the enablers will usually find expression in behaviours at every level of relationship. Difficulty can move out in ever-widening ripples, affecting individual families, organizations and ultimately nations. Some of the signs that we are into harmful emotional climates are obvious to us, yet linking these emotions to unmet needs and doing something about it may still lie outside our awareness.

Some can cluster around nurture, others around esteem and so on. The compound effect of deficits in development can create hurt that can harden into patterns and be passed on across generations.

Re-enabling needs

The *5 Enablers* at their optimal levels will indeed build the wherewithal for creative outflow.

Develomental issues in these enablers may be visited again and again, each time finding a new nuance or even a fresh trigger for growth and change. Our own learning readiness will improve as we gain increasing awareness. So take a pen, make notes, have conversations, challenge these ideas and test them out in your relationships. Building more awareness and skill in all *5 Enablers* will help ease conflict in any form of negotiation. In part 3 we will see how, but for now we will revisit the third Essential – Respect of Differences. We will see first, how having a deeper understanding about differences will form a vital part in our quest to stay creative.

CHAPTER 9
UNDERSTANDING DIFFERENCES

Why it matters

Part of what helps us stay in a creative flow with others is the ability to see beyond surface differences. To deepen our understanding of the natural tension that arises in the complex terrain of dealing with differences, we need to expand our view.

In the well-worn but apposite phrase, we either become part of the solution or part of the problem.

Diversity is a given and the trend of globalization means that every facet of living co-operatively requires the creative input of each of us, so that we can 'enlarge' and meaningfully approach problem solving. Tension in the face of difference runs the full gamut, from excitement to fear. Tension is inherent in the movement of life. Weathering this natural response is a challenge facing each of us.

We need helpful tension to get us going, to get energised and into life. Tension arises most acutely in difference, and affects each and every one of us because, as humans, we are so porous - our sensory system is constantly sensing our environment.

Few of us take seriously enough the fact that, as organic interconnected beings, we constantly cross-fertilize with one another. This cross-fertilizing offers us the gift of relationship that makes connection and progress possible. With this comes a wide spectrum of emotional responses. A natural frisson occurs when we encounter difference. We enjoy some differences and find them exciting - here all is well. Yet when we are challenged by differences, we have usually bypassed that frisson of excitement, here the contrast of differences bring mismatch and perhaps friction or fear. When differences provoke fear it is only a short hop to conflict. However, when we can begin to trust the view that difference is the raw material and impetus for change and variety, we begin to make progress, side-stepping any tendency to escalate the tension and, instead, learning new ways of including our differences.

Twenty-first century challenge

We live in an age where eruptions of destructive power struggles threaten to contaminate the trust that is vital to creativity. Worldwide, festering tensions have led to the discontent and rage that fuels terrorism - the acts of people who no longer believe in the sense of fair play. The perception of what makes for fair play may, of course, be accurate or inaccurate - reasonable or irrational. However the thinking, feeling and behaviours that flow from perceptions are potentially just as dangerous, whether the perception is real or imagined - fair or unfair. To feel threatened or to feel treated unjustly can damage us in our heart, our mind, our body and our spirit, causing us to experience the type of fear that is grist to the wheels of conflict.

When tensions rise

When we have no understanding of the fears that arise from differences and the meaning of that fear in our lives, everyday issues can become unmanageable and attitudes can harden. The greater the tension the more we are tipped towards conflict and divisiveness. Conflict can eclipse our common humanity, and as it does the greater difficulty we have in being stress-hardy to life's ordinary tensions. Heightened sensitivity can reach levels where the slightest stimuli will cause pain and worsening rigidity. Possibility for respectful relating, for transformation and healing, are difficult ideals to keep alive when conflict worsens. Despairing onlookers to conflict situations often comment that the issues seem trivial or petty.

Unfair treatment and injustice grow out of these circumstances. Resolution can seem far from reach and force and harshness can be a norm. When this happens our responses become toxic and contagious to those involved, moving out in ever-widening circles. In conflict, the type of response we have often runs a spectrum of extremes, from passive to aggressive. An extreme response of either is likely to play out, cause escalation and avoidance. Responses vary in keeping with temperament and experience. Extremes of either response can be devastating, causing 'lash out' or 'shut down'; at critical mass we have potential for serious conflict.

When there are enough people with a personal axe to grind, it can find expression in 'a cause or a war.' The demonizing of the 'other side' and systematic withholding of human rights sets the scene for both sides.

All wars arise when people cannot communicate and dialogue breaks down. Fighting and war-making produce a winner and a loser. In its turn, this contributes and lays the foundations for future fighting.

In aggression, desperate efforts to be rid of tensions are made to banish the view of one side or the other. Domination and subjugation, or annihilation, can become a prevailing and governing pattern. Where this happens we are into real and serious trouble. In passivity we may appease, become indifferent or despair, unable or unwilling to encounter the realities of the conflict we face. And when such tensions build, fear levels disrupt trust. Rebuilding trust and diffusing hostilities can take generations.

Tension in the face of difference, it seems, is the last thing we want to have around us. We moan that it is unfair when we are faced with it - try as we do - and escape is impossible. As soon as we give it a slip in one place, it arrives to meet us elsewhere. For many of us this is bound to create problems.

To be human, it seems, we each inherit our share of helpful and unhelpful responses to the tensions that turn to frictions. We may snarl at it, repress it and attempt 'once and for all' strikes in order to destroy it - but back it bounces. With this approach our commonality is eclipsed. We become divisive and are tipped back into an 'us or them' mentality that ensures conflict. Naturally, conflict brings feelings of hate; we want to expel what we perceive as the source of our troubles.

To defuse the dangers of vigorous hatred, we need to understand what is really going on. Where choices are made to build trust, a steady and widespread surge of creative energy can become the norm. Building trust is often painstaking, yet more than anything else it is the condition that gets flexibility going, and lets creativity flow freely.

Humanitarian principals for a more trusting and creative world can seem inadequate against the fierceness of hate responses.

In the suggestion that love is slow-burning there is a seed of hope, implying as it does that, over time, albeit in small ways, where we can build trust, the conditions for love are made. For real love has an enduring quality that can bring a settlement, when hate reaches burn-out. It is easy to feel cynical and to doubt. It can even be convenient, as it can free us from all further requirements to involve ourselves. Yet, any meaningful resolution of hatred will involve a rethink about the way we each individually understand and handle our conflicts. To look closely at the deeper issues behind the positions taken is the only way to win hearts and minds, to develop what we need.

Beyond difficulty with difference

To deal effectively with difference we must work with it - we must commit to the combination of your part and mine. *We can make together* is a winning formula that helps increase co-operation. We get more than the sum of your part and mine when we combine and use our difference - we get value added, we get synergy. So difference and mismatch are normal. Without acceptance of this overarching fact of life, ruptures can easily set in.

We can take it that within certain ranges we each negotiate fairly well. Some of us may not be challenged by gender difference yet find value differences difficult; others have a hard time with the time warps or lag in intergenerational or intercultural issues - and others remain unconscious of their level of difference intolerance. Many of us do fine in our own little bubble. Yet, beyond our well-learned coping mechanisms, and outside our home circles, whenever we feel threatened it's fair to say that we will be less surefooted or safe. When we meet differences that challenge, it moves us off the familiar - and often fear is waiting in the wings. How well we react to this fear makes or breaks the outcome of our dealings.

Conflict and creativity

In truth all of us are capable of both creativity and conflict in the face of feeling the tension inherent in differences. There is always an oncoming stream of different needs, desires and challenges to be negotiated in every sphere of life. Gaps between our ideals and the reality of our lives can cause high stress and tensions, leading to problems.

Because we live in a complex world, where grappling with a mass of stimuli is the norm, naturally differences that arise can be testing. Yet it will keep us alert, engaged and energized. Frustration, challenge and growing pains will also surface as we make the transitions that are part of living creatively. Embracing differences will keep us alive and deepen our compassion. Naturally, the more we adapt, flex and live with differences, the better we become at being truly human. Destructive fights lock us into right and wrong - good and bad. Getting past such attitudes is really worth working for. It will also involve us in a more honest encounter with the deeper levels of our own being.

Shadow

The Russian philosopher and dissident, Aleksandr Solzhenitsyn, pointed to the complexity by saying:
"If only there were evil people somewhere insidiously committing evil deeds, and it were necessary only to separate them from the rest of us and destroy them, but the line dividing good and evil cuts through the heart of every human being."

'Shadow' was a term coined by psychologist Carl Jung to describe the denied and hidden aspects of ourselves.

Shadow can be viewed as the hurting, fearful and unloved side of the human personality. It is in the realm of this shadowy unconscious that festering upsets reside. When these turn into hatreds, resistances, guilt complexes and jealousies they can spill out here and there when some event presses a trigger. If we each took care of our own share of shadow, we would not need to project it onto others. We would be able to integrate shadow safely, if we understood that at base, it is the benign unmet needs, misunderstandings and fears that lie hidden in it. Such stuff gets to be unhelpful when we are unconscious of its power and lack the supports and skills to harness and understand it. When we engage with these deeper issues, we learn that they can be our teacher; they can carry a deeper message.

Once we can start to integrate and be responsible for how to live well, we move away from the right or wrong projections and no longer make others the bad guys - the black sheep who must carry shadow in mega quantities.

We all have a shadow - a side that we fear to own and feel. Our tendency is to fragment, disown and project such feared parts onto others rather than accepting and taking responsibility for them. Understandably we are each at our own particular stage of understanding, courage and development. Yet we get to be more creative by owning and integrating all aspects of ourselves, warts and all. And when we do, the simplistic 'us and them' thinking won't do. The more we take responsibility to be informed about our own part, the sooner we can make positive change. We get to be less conflictual and we let our creativity flow.

Once again, imagine if we became fully conscious and changed our approach. If we were to commit ourselves to connecting with others, cross-fertilizing our ideas, we could stay on the side of possibility and improve our lives immensely. Indeed, a great deal of conflict in the world could be lessened or healed by promoting personal empowerment and harnessing the creative power in people. In recognising the tension inherent in differences as part of the grand scheme in the renewal process, differences can be more readily viewed as the valuable raw material of innovation and evolution. Difference can then be seen as a stimulus to creativity somewhat in the way the challenging pebble in an oyster proves a necessary part of making a pearl.

Mindful creativity

"Openness to different points of view is an important aspect of being mindfully creative," says psychologist Ellen J. Langer in her book, *On Becoming an Artist*. Once we become mindfully aware of views other than our own, she adds, we start to realize that there are many points of view and that this awareness will liberate us.

Langer warns against polarising right and wrong, and gives an example of how differing perspectives change what something means to us. "A steer may be a steak to a rancher, a sacred object to a Hindu, a collection of genes and proteins to a molecular biologist." We need, she suggests, to "remain aware that the number of possible perspectives will never be exhausted."

Langer goes further to explain that, although this promotes uncertainty, that same uncertainty leads to mindfulness. We need not worry because "uncertainty promotes opportunity to learn ... recognising the power of uncertainty allows us to grow and promotes a dynamic, rather than a static, relationship with our world." Uncertainty can be very challenging, even provoking feelings of crises, yet crises can be negotiated and transformed into opportunity.

The hurt that flows from conflict affects not just ourselves but those around us. When it reaches toxic levels, it makes life more burdensome and pressured than it need be. Wounds can play out in the plethora of behaviours that flow from power struggles. These behaviours are often nothing more than misguided attempts to protect a basic need that has gone unmet. When needs for survival, security, dignity, belonging and expression are threatened, we are all capable of behaving in ways that would seem alien to us when we have these guaranteed.

Making sense of our humanity for the most part involves getting a handle on the possibility that personal empowerment can build trust. When we learn to build trust, fears can be integrated and normalized. The problem with a lack of conscious awareness of how creative we can be is that we fail to make inroads on doing all we can to draw it out. Wounds that accrue from loss and lack can lead to behaviours that narrow and sabotage a full and creative life.

When we are ready to understand our fears we stop denying our hurts and take charge of making some changes. Yet when we disown our fears we become blind to their driving force.

Where to from here?

We have established that the *3 Essentials* - creative awareness, needs enablement and respect of differences - are the mix that must take root before creativity can thrive.

In Part One we began to understand how the essentials empower creativity. In Part Two we saw that shortfall occurs for most, that healing is a personal growth task and that change is always possible. By now we know that, to unleash our creativity, we must believe in it - we must become empowered to negotiate our needs and, finally, we must learn to honour diversity by being inclusive. Although each aspect has been highlighted individually, in reality the trio of essentials are the master trust-builders that unleash our creativity. They mingle, cross-fertilize and encourage us to expand our horizons. They play out daily within the complexity of life's rich tapestry, challenging us to greater levels of understanding. When we can harmonise this mix, we can indeed ease conflict.

As we move into Part three, we will see how we can negotiate with a creative, rather than conflictual, approach. We will take a deeper look at how our normal human tendencies can, in the face of threat, rush us into fight or flight.

We will also see how primal fear of loss can fuel the intense emotions that send people into the type of behaviour that underpins toxic conflict. We will look more closely at how opening our heart and using our head can bring ease to conflict and promote creativity in all our encounters.

Finally, we will learn how the mediator employs tried and tested rational and emotional principles to build trust; how unravelling the message in the emotion can de-escalate the fears that close our hearts to creative resolution.

PART THREE

A HEART AND HEAD APPROACH

CHAPTER 10

NEGOTIATING – A HEART AND HEAD APPROACH

The importance of self-awareness in negotiation

It is hardly surprising that our level of self-awareness will show up in negotiations. The degree of understanding about interpersonal relationship can make or break virtually every transaction. When we aspire to be creative in our negotiations, we aim to be true, congruent and tuned into our own and others' best potential. In this we begin to sustain the hope that our differing needs will be genuinely expressed, respected and traded. As we achieve even a modicum of success we empower a creative attitude that, in time, can become our norm. Things would move more slowly if we really took seriously the challenge to become more conscious of how we negotiate. Yet this can have a positive influence in the long run.

Negotiation skills tend to be taught in business schools and are traditionally and predominantly in the realm of work-related activities. We need to continue to focus on the idea that negotiation is a life skill so that we can be more artful negotiators in every sphere of life.

All conflict can be seen as a 'wake up' call to the fact that negotiation is needed. On a day-by-day basis, as we aim to live creatively in a diverse landscape, we must learn to stay true to what it takes to meet the needs of ourselves and others; this is in essence the imperative of best practice from the world of negotiation. Easing conflict becomes possible when, as negotiators, we can practice the 3 *Essentials* that form the backbone of this book. Let us recap quickly on the essentials because, as we have seen, they are the scaffolding on which we build the sustainable creativity that will bring ease to the inevitable conflicts that are part of life.

Essentials for easing conflict

At some point during the mediation process, those participants who successfully conclude with agreement will discover three things. They will find that they actually have the wherewithal within themselves to create a fair outcome; they realise that, as needs are objectively identified, they can be seen to be valid for each person involved; and, lastly, as they begin to honour that difference is part of life's diversity. When the 3 *Essentials* dawn, the parties can settle down and lessen the fear spirals that come from trying to impose a one-sided view of what a good outcome would look like.

With Essential 1...
... we have a belief in the renewing creative core that is in all of us; this gives us the power to persevere in the face of difficulty and to reach successful outcomes.

With Essential 2...
... we can see the spectrum of human needs; the *5 Enablers* are part and parcel of what is essential to creativity.

With Essential 3...
... we will honour the principle that differences are valuable as progenitors of change, innovation and complementariness.

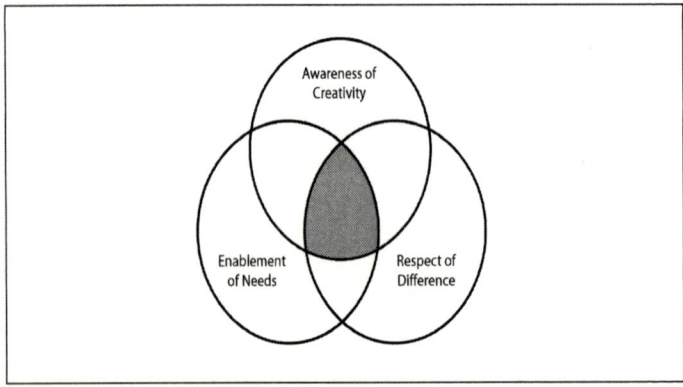

The spirit of creativity that flows from these essentials will help us view life through a wider lens, to flex and adapt. But it is not perfection. Far from it- negotiating life with all its differences is, by nature, highly challenging. To live is to be subject to ups and downs, yet creativity nudges us to love the good in life, to handle the natural sorrows of loss, to be real, resilient and renewing. Conflicts arise when we find ourselves in opposition with one another or, indeed, when two aspects of something are out of balance and competing for dominance. Force and counter-force leads to power struggle. However when negotiations are aligned with principles of creativity, we have an attitude that lets us be objective about facts and aware of feelings. It lets us envision possibilities and set about doing what is practical.

Building bridges

A mediator gives time and makes space for people who have chosen to search for a way to bridge their divisions. The mediation process creates a structure where participants can explore their fears of loss and invest their creative energy in shaping their future relationship. Within this process, the aim is to find ways of moving forward - ways of avoiding the pitfalls of an *us or them* attitude that can so easily escalate into a *win-lose* destructive conflict. In the process, the emphasis is on a search for mutuality; for win-win solutions.

Confronting conflict head-on tends to produce a win-lose climate, triggering fear of loss with all its implications for reactive fight and flight responses. An effort is made to create an overarching atmosphere of inclusiveness that lets each side make connections by telling their stories, each from their own perspectives. In this, metaphorical bridges are made and mutuality becomes possible. A bridge brings parties together to put forward their arguments, envision options and create understanding. By sincere commitment each can gradually learn the principles that maintain integrity; moreover they will learn to listen, clarify and broaden awareness of each other's heartfelt emotional views. With bridges we can trade, cross-fertilize, complement, resource and strengthen each other - when we do, we are promoting creativity. When fears put up barriers they block bridges - and the cross-connections that let us communicate, collaborate and support one another cease. When this happens, the energy exchange for creative expansion is extinguished. Without bridges cut-offs occur and allow closure to other points of view. In extreme, rigidities and hostilities can easily set in. Again, where this happens we may well be on course for conflict rather than creativity.

Where bridges exist, people can make connections and use their combined energies to make progress.

Being on the bridge is a great privilege when a mediator gets to facilitate the changes required to bring on vitality, renewal and innovation. The skill of the mediator is to engage deeply at an emotional level, without losing sight of the key principles that empower creativity in people, or to get blinded by the emotional crises.

Crises and opportunity

Interestingly, the Chinese use the same symbol for crisis as they do for opportunity. It is the tensions of differences that are the spur for expansion and problem-solving. Change and growth happens in the small tracks and traces of everyday life. This is exactly as it needs to be. Life is multi-faceted and richly textured; it offers infinite encounters in which to learn. Yet, all of us have parts of ourselves that respond by being creative and parts where the everyday conflicts trip us up and bog us down again. To ease conflict we must move our focus on to our common human bonds, to the things that bind us, rather than to what it is that separates us. The mediator learns the art of easing conflict over time with practice and knowledge. Learning from the mediator's art will ask us to stay with the tensions of the situation, to engage fully and to pace our negotiations in a more conscious way.

Beginning negotiations, especially where pressures exist, will involve holding possibility for good outcomes. This helps provide energy to stay, engage and pace discussions.

Working to resolve conflict

A mediator truly interested in the art of easing conflict uses an approach that is systemic, organic and collaborative. It is person-centred in that it challenges people to encounter each other, to have dialogue, to meet and to take the emotional risk of being real.

This does not, however, preclude structure, parameters and boundaries. To live without structures would take us into chaos. Balancing flow and structure is best achieved by being conscious of both.

The spirit of mediation

The emphasis in this book is about having a deeper understanding of what we need in order to be creative and ease our conflicts. The kernel of negotiation theory, I feel, has been put forward by Ury and Fisher in declaring that "negotiators are people first" and advising that we can be hard on issues, but we must be soft with people.

It is simple at one level, yet ultimately it challenges us to a more sophisticated form of relating.

Using all our faculties

To be human is to have a range of faculties. Being aware and tapping into them is very empowering in our negotiations, big or small. Thinking helps make informed decisions, feeling helps us to be caring, spirit ensures hope, and doing makes it happen. By harnessing the power of all our faculties we begin to experience real empowerment. Engaging all our faculties gives us the makings of a truly holistic approach. The range of faculties includes:

Spiritual: gives us the ability to use meditation, imagination, intuition and aspiration.

Intellectual: gives us the ability to think things through, get information, measure, compare, reason, set goals and make decisions.

Emotional: gives us the ability to empathize with feelings and to experience our emotions; our joy, sorrow, love, hate, fear, anger, gratitude, forgiveness and regret.

Material: gives us the ability to make concrete the practicalities of life. To get into action, practising, making and shaping the form of our reality.

The faculties combined

All four faculties working together can help the modern problem-solver. Conscious development of each, linkage between them and the coming together of all four strands may well be what it takes to promote future development, in ways that ensure our evolution as humans. We may now have entered a time when to be stuck in just one mode will leave us fragmented or narrow in our approach. To be stuck in thinking mode may remove us to an ivory tower; to be stuck in feeling mode may overwhelm; to be stuck in spiritual mode may lack grounding; and to be stuck in practical may make us busy without progress. All four, of course, are completely necessary, but again when it comes to easing conflict, consciousness and balance are the transformative keys.

Solutions that come via a process of engaging all four faculties tend to be wise, broad and generous. To learn more about this, one book by Myers and Briggs with the great title of *Gifts Differing* is helpful. In it the authors demonstrate how we can be valuing of all faculties, and how an understanding of these human gifts will make us more effective.

Using all our facilities actually helps us to keep heart and hold our head in the face of challenging difficulties.

Head and heart - emotional and rational

Before we begin negotiations of any kind it may well be worth asking what kind of process we are hoping for. What would make for a good outcome? What kind of checklist might we use to keep us creative? How do we go about bringing solutions that can be seen to have the hallmark of integrity and substance? Negotiation that is truly principled aims at its broadest to promote the rational and the emotional – sometimes called a heart and head approach. This two-fold process brings together the structures and processes that build a sense of fairness that can be tested both subjectively and objectively. It feels fair and can be seen to be fair. Resolve that holds is more likely when the decisions we make in our negotiations take both into consideration. In mediation the skill set is to begin to bring both the rational and the emotional together.

Robert Benjamin, an American mediator, debunked the dichotomy of settling personal and business disputes in differing ways. Benjamin had this to say about transforming conflict: "Virtually every conflict - be it a business or a family dispute - has subjective, non-rational aspects that must be addressed. In fact, many business conflicts are in essence personal disputes in disguise or in drag, if you will. A disputing party almost always has a personal and emotional stake in the outcome. At base, virtually every conflict is personal."

To stay creative, it seems, we must acknowledge that heart and head are linked; informing, and cross-informing each other in ongoing cycles. Bringing heart and head to the task will produce more than the sum of the parts. It will open doors and make us effective. Making this connection keeps negotiations fluid, flexible and fair.

Opening up to heart and head

To be rational asks for abstraction, objectivity and measure. These help us to examine the factors that will help achieve problem solving. The skill to partialize problems, to break them down to manageable size, to gain information and make an assessment can all help us to make more informed choices - to stay with issues and to chart change. Not surprisingly, any inputs that help us to become more emotionally literate will help us understand what lies behind our emotions. Becoming emotionally engaged gives us a connection to the deeper meaningful inner compass that will be part of working through the life choices that seem caring, kind and meaningful to us.

Over time I have come to understand that, when the creative flow that allows for real option development is blocked, it is usually caused by an emotional arrest. Fear of loss either closes off or floods the arena of the heart. This limits possibility because it is from the heart that our most beneficent outflow of hopes, desires and aspirations arise. Understanding the information encoded in our emotions helps modulate, decode and prevent overwhelm. It also gives us the fluency that helps to make our responses more flexible. This promotes perseverance and helps rationalise plans for the practicalities that can be translated into the behavioural steps necessary to make good our ideas, hopes and goals.

I mediated a situation some time ago where a couple actually cared a lot about each other. Let me call them R and J. They, in fact, wanted to stay in their relationship. They worked for over a year, separately at first, on what had been a power struggle of approaches - whether to lead with the heart or head. Each seemed to dismiss the validity of the other. In reality, it is more likely that an eclipse had taken place. R, favouring a very rational approach, often refused to allow feelings to surface in decision making. J, who would only deal in emotion, refused to allow rational approaches to problem solving. After they had once again committed to their relationship, I received a call from R. He said that he had found of late that he was much more able to meet on an emotional basis. He was actually more open-hearted in his approach and, what is more, he really felt much better in himself. I asked what he thought had changed and how. He said that it was when the rational side of his approach was seen, validated and respected that he had managed to move on; to put his heart into the equation. J when I spoke with her confirmed that their relating had improved. Both had become more appreciative of each other's overt style, she told me, and she had begun to understand that behind the very emotional nature she displayed, she too valued a rational approach. Both parts, when acknowledged, can create a synergy that will fuel ongoing creativity. Excluding either heart or head can slow progress in our negotiations.

Where a heart and head approach is honoured, we can start to develop and exchange in ways that enhance each other. When we do, we add to the creative quotient in the world.

The interface of heart and head - it's the place to be

When we bring both heart and head together we can think through the practicalities while staying in touch with the feelings that humanise us. It is sometimes said that the heart is wise and the head is knowledge-able, that the heart can muddle through where the head would despair. Perhaps ? Yet, by attempting to honour both, we set up the conditions it takes for the ongoing task of bringing ease to our conflicts. The art involved increases as we get accomplished in negotiat-ing in ways that respect both heart and head. Because they are constantly interacting in every transaction, not surprisingly, the interface where both heart and head meet is where we must locate.

Generally speaking, a successful marriage of heart and head will be found in a fair accommodation of both the practical and the emotional. Resolve is an ongoing process of negotiation, subject always to changes that make it necessary to flex and weave within the ins and outs of living. It is subject to flow and ebb. In flow we move readily; in ebb we must stop to take a deeper look. In acknowledging the complexity of modern living, we develop a wider lens through which to view things and in doing so we further our understanding. Where fairness is thought and felt to be important, we learn to engage our heart and head in all types of negotiation.

So often, though, we see our heart and head as separate and give little conscious effort to use both in our negotiations. We may have developed a persona that polarises one or other; we may refuse to connect heart and head; we may invalidate one or other, believing in the rational to the exclusion of the emotional, or *vice versa*. How well we develop a self that can engage both heart and head will have a bearing on the soundness of our negotiations.

At the start of this book I said that during the years I have been a mediator I have been struck by how quickly people learn to negotiate when the spirit of fairness is held to be important. Many of us stay 'stuck' with problems all because we are not aware of the basics that underpin all of life's negotiations - we don't know where to start. Consciously or unconsciously, each day we get out of bed we face a spectrum of negotiations. It is natural to want a fair share of the things that nurture us. To have food, shelter, warmth and so forth. We also want to feel safe, to be included, to be respected and to have a meaningful livelihood. When we can see that fairness goes hand-in-hand with sustainable progress, we become able to take the gradual, regular and sometimes imperfect steps that map our journeys through the complex territory of negotiation.

Validity of needs

When we see that legitimate needs can be asserted and negotiated we begin to experience ease. Moving off any tendency to find fault, we learn that we have a right to a fair share of the nurture that ensures our survival, even when resources are limited. We have a right to feel safe. We have a right to our dignity. We have a right to feel we belong. We have a right to feel empowered to express our authentic self.. We have a right to make and shape a creative life. Negotiating our conflicts is always dynamic. In practising the art of easing conflict, all of us need to keep a caring focus on solutions, take time to unravel what lies behind the conflict. It is human to fear losing out on what we need.

With more understanding of the needs template that are human rights, we can be both emotional and rational in ways that help negotiate - in ways that are fair. When we become aware that these universal needs come via our human nature, we get to understand that meeting them brings us to our highest creativity. We possess within ourselves the impetus to have these needs met; it is not selfish but serves humanity. When we come fully into our best, we can map out creative solutions in whichever negotiation we encounter. Doing our part to promote trust within our own circles can help promote healthy relationship.

Transforming conflict is largely a matter of working in a timely way to identify, balance and negotiate needs. To begin to negotiate with an intention to win at the expense of another is power playing rather than principled negotiation. Many of the roots of our conflicts lie in problems in our baseline experiences with the *5 Enablers*. We will find in one way or another that they are the deep interests behind the positions we take in our negotiations. Being clear about them will bring success.

(Re-read at your ease the *5 Enablers* in part 2)

These needs as we have seen are the block-builders of creativity. All five set the scene for what it takes to be creative in our negotiations. Because when our *nurture needs* are recognized, we can share more easily. When our *security needs* are recognized, we can venture forward to take a chance more easily. When our *need to belong* is recognized we can live inclusively. We more readily become a player and accept the interdependence of relationship. When our *esteem needs* are recognized we can value one another. We can accept the core innate dignity of individuals, beyond the behaviours or circumstances of our conflicts. When we develop capability we have the skill to contribute to making progress.

We also saw how loss of needs takes us into unhealthy patterns that generate fears. When needs are blocked, frustrated and ignored, serious damage can occur. When fear around needs abound, they set in train behaviours that are devious at best and destructive at worst. Behaviours that seek to create external 'power over' are based on fears around needs.

There may be an actual injustice, or a sense of threat looming in relation to our needs. When we look at negotiating our conflicts we must always look to the wounded world of unmet needs. It is the central focus for any mediation; it cannot be overstressed that the personal needs of our inner landscape will find expression, consciously or unconsciously, in the day-to-day negotiations of life.

Within the arena of mediation, where person-centered negotiation that honours heart and head is practised, a change comes about as the five enabling needs for promoting creativity are learned and put into action. As parties regain hope, acknowledge their differences and focus their negotiations on the mutuality of needs, the 'overwhelm effect' from the force or blockage of conflict is avoided and we can have the experience of playing fair.

As we engage heart and head we begin to seek out fairness. We begin to communicate in a clear, conscious and collaborative spirit in our negotiations.

Building consensus by accommodating arguments, including various points of view and staying in dialogue will require that we keep a careful eye on fairness.

To stay true to the principles that release sustainable creativity, we must learn to negotiate in ways that are experienced as fair. In the next chapter we will see what we must grapple with in order to stay fair.

CHAPTER 11

A SEARCH FOR FAIRNESS

Fairness is just another word for balance. It seeks out a golden mean that can harmonise the day-to-day necessities of living. We balance our transactions through complementary give and take, through mutuality and trading.

Fairness attempts to be even-handed in transactions. Fairness is subjective yet it can often be measured objectively also. In seeking it, we are always promoting ethical frames of reference. Fairness aims to respect integrity and resources.

When we successfully negotiate conflict, we honour the right to hold different views; we aim to meet needs and we hold to the possibility that we have within us the capacity to create mutuality in outcomes.

Weathering the natural tensions as we move to implement these essentials is then a challenge for each of us. When we doubt our creative ability, when the hope of meeting our legitimate needs is threatened, and when differences divide rather than complement, we will have difficulty staying fair in our negotiations. Mismatch of views and scarce resources in the 'here and now' will generate tensions. Power plays can sabotage lasting agreement. Creative solutions usually come about when the spirit of mutual empowerment is learned and honoured. Without this awareness we may miss out on fair play.

Where the sustainable creative power of fair play, a power that honours the integrity of all individuals, is denied we are territory where more devious forms of abusive power can surface.

Recognising Power Abuse

Fair negotiations are sabotaged if we enshrine power imbalances and fail to ask how they can be redressed.

Power balancing is a major factor in professional mediation. Balancing the integrity and resources within negotiation is the guiding spirit of the mediator. Allowing arguments to be put forward, to state and restate, review and agree on ways forward is, in fact, all part of our legitimate power base as human beings. Keeping negotiations constructive is part of the process that allows continuous dialogue, Sometimes we move straight into blame, *'cut offs'* and even punishment with no awareness of what it might have taken to resolve the conflict. Power struggles lead us to fight in ways that oppose one another, exclude one another, and deny one another. Systematic maintenance of these behaviours is the executioner of creativity. Opposing, excluding and denying trigger conflict. That said, in our day-to-day reality there is such a strong belief that contest rather than collaboration is the spur for living. When contest is the dominant view, a winner versus loser is the viewfinder we operate from, and it can be very difficult to believe that it is possible to choose otherwise and still achieve our genuinely held interests.

Power struggling is very common. In our attempts for equilibrium, for balance, it is not hard to want to meet what we perceive as dangerous with force, abandonment or denial. Yet trust is eroded when we engage any one of these.

The variety of ways we engage power is subject to gargantuan levels of information; power plays within society are very complex as the 'how, what and why' of power can be baffling. Knowing the power base that operates can help short-circuit inflammatory missives. The desire for power over others is the greatest danger to sustainable creativity. Transparency that leads to acknowledging how power is being played out is obviously valued when it comes to promoting the negotiations that lead to creativity.

Those that are open and clear are easily understood; for instance, the power of expertise may come into play as we negotiate on a day-to-day basis. We have the power of authority in the role we carry. We can have veto power, nuisance power, or the power of persuasion. Perhaps, too, we have referent power - the power of linkages with established power-bases in politics or the power of being with a winning team and so on. We may accumulate power or 'piggyback' on power. The permutations go on. Some power bases are dubious because they are unsustainable. When power is played out competitively it erodes the opportunity to have a level playing field. It sets in train, me against you, and you against me. Essentially, this sets up a power play mentality that over time can hold vast reserves of energy trapped in the struggle for a 'win.' It is hardly necessary to say that this erodes trust and leads to an interplay that fuels a win-lose climate. Certainly, unless we have some understanding of the usefulness of questioning how we play power, what we are aiming to gain and why, we may lack real understanding.

A power struggle is most often a maladaptive attempt to have legitimate needs heard, respected and met. Most of us can be blinded by our own passions, often making for more heat than light in negotiations. We can feel that we must force what is 'right' and that to give in to another seems to make no sense. Frustrations can have us screaming inside for revenge. Unfortunately, this is not the best way. It is not sustainable because anything that is disempowering to another will not further ongoing relationship.

This is why fights often take on a repetitive quality. To sort out difficulty in a more enduring way there is nothing for it but to return to an understanding of the first principles of what keeps us creative and what it is that tips us into conflict. Adopting an extreme may be an attempt by an overwhelmed and frightened ego state to survive. When we adopt a stance of 'power over,' rather than the more sustainable personal empowerment, behaviours are driven by a need to control. As a controlling mode takes hold it hardens into patterns so that personal empowerment is diminished, and with it goes the opportunity for sustainable creativity. In the face of things that threaten we can feel that we are disempowered and, very naturally, we can be alerted into primal fear responses. When we are unaware, we can be provoked reactively. The power of fair play in negotiations operates in the knowledge that balancing needs is what will make a sustainable power base in society. Fairness is inherently understood when we experience it. As we get more aware of how power plays operate, how both lack and excess of power serves to trigger the intense responses that fuel conflict, it can help to clear a space for real talks to take place - those that bring heart and head together.

When we become more competent negotiators, we stop playing destructive games that keep us in unconscious cycles of fight and flight. As we begin to understand more about what our real needs amount to, we learn to identify them, set goals and understand what our emotional responses are all about. We begin to negotiate from the principle of heart and head.

Principled negotiation

Principled negotiation has a spirit that is collaborative. With commitment we can learn to negotiate in ways that promote the development of flexible, creatively-charged people who aim to be fair. Our common humanity imbues a thread that enables a capacity for empathy. It is a universal understanding that, unless distorted by trauma, tends to serve us well when building trust. Conflicts that are entrenched are our greatest danger, because, over time, they eclipse trust with hateful fears. Those fears might be real or imagined, yet they ring alarm bells. Getting down to talking with one another, sharing hopes and concerns, and sifting through these, is the essence of what brings about transformative change.

Communication

Ideally during collaborative negotiations, a two-way exchange lets us interact with one another. Effective communication will let us say our piece in a way that gives our views on the issues before us. It will also ask us to hear, acknowledge the views of others. Effective communication then is largely about expressing what we have to say and listening to what is being expressed to us. The goal of communication is to hear and be heard. When we are clear in our communication we can make a more informed response. Being able to share information clearly and directly, while, at the same time, handling our emotions is a crucial part of communication. Effective communication can help us receive another's reality without being overwhelmed by it. For this reason, when it comes to negotiation, understanding how to learn from and stay with our emotional cues will be vital.

Simple as this seems, it is very important to be able to handle our feelings in a given situation. Speaking and listening, hearing and being heard, are all enriched, amplified and complicated to lesser or greater degree by our emotions. We may walk away from situations because know-how falls short and talks break down. Many of us move too quickly from 'feeling' to 'action.' cutting out the process of looking at things and exploring our feelings. Reactivity can create havoc. Easing conflict will ask us to be proactive rather than reactive. In seeking to create solutions, rather than jumping into knee-jerk emotional reactions, we are exercising a choice about our responses. Being more switched on to what emotions are all about will make it easier. Living reactively often limits creative empowerment. Because living reactively excludes making more informed choice. Bernard Mayer is a Canadian mediator and writer. In his book, The Dynamics of Conflict Resolution he tells us that "The best communication occurs when people are genuine and natural. Communication is about interacting as human beings. This means being real, being oneself, speaking from the heart, and connecting with others on the basis of human personalities, which by definition is flawed." He also suggests "tolerance of people's difficulty in communicating (including your own) is essential".

Finding the words to say what we feel and having information about the rights that dignify life will help with effective communication. Finding a way to say something can be important. Sometimes it can be tone that matters. Taking the insulting voltage out of comments will often involve taking time out to cool down, to process emotions. The situation may also call for a protection - a power balancing structure perhaps. Whatever will help with communication is well worth encouraging. Communicating congruently what we need, how we feel, while being able to empathise with others' needs and feelings, is part of what we do to bring ease to conflict. In reality, within our everyday negotiations there are situations where mismatch will create impasse, blockage and a need to re-route. Facing this reality is part of what makes us effective negotiators.

Facing challenges:
possibility versus limitation

Everywhere in life's negotiations we are confronted with both possibility and limitation. Possibility encourages us towards exploration and expansion while limitation asks us to practice acceptance, to remain with 'what is.' Our challenge in all our negotiations is to 'dance' between holding on and letting go. All effective negotiation will involve an element of holding on and giving way, of asserting and yielding.

We cannot be a player in life without the ability to assert - to put forward. The ability to yield and step back is of equal importance. In our assertiveness we ask for the opportunity to put our arguments, view points and concerns. In yielding we step back and include the views of others; we factor in their concerns. Getting stuck in extremes of either creates imbalances that in time may limit effective negotiation. Saying yes, saying no, accepting and rejecting, are all part of our repertoire as good negotiators. Learning to hold on, learning to let go, is part of the intrinsic life dance. We must do our best to live out our hopes yet, alongside this, we must also learn to accept that, when we have done all we can, we gracefully let go of any tendency to force change or to punish. We withdraw and keep our energy focussed on re-routing, new terms and fresh possibility. Time without outer activity, can bring the calm space for reflection that allows new options to percolate. Simply by staying true to this organic way of relating, by trusting innate creativity, fostering a healthy balance of needs and respecting the right to hold differing views - by staying true to the search for connections and letting go when the time seems right - our way of relating becomes more harmonious. When we can do this we are adding to a creative future. The diversity, colour and creativity innate in us can shine through. This will mean the world to the next generation.

Beyond power struggle

Mediation opens up the opportunity to exchange views, meet needs fairly and take responsibility for staying with possibility. By engaging in this process, all involved work to lessen the toxicity of power struggles and bring ease to the conflict at hand. For many, the relationship balance sheet may need harmonising. Energy exchange is always attempting to achieve equilibrium. This is not to encourage a narrow tit for tat attitude about exchange in relationship, indeed conscious generosity, sacrifice and gift is part and parcel of life. However it is important to have awareness that if we relate unfairly, something will eventually disrupt relationship. A search for fairness is always being reckoned in our negotiations. In her book on Chinese culture, *Watching the Tree,* Adeline Yen Mah describes the concept of Mei Mei or Buy/Sell. She says it is always at play: "If the transaction is perceived by either party as lopsided or unfair, if one side has to 'eat losses' too many times, the Buy/Sell will fail and the relationship will eventually end. It is as simple as that."

True creativity is sustainable when we appreciate the need for balances. Principled negotiation can help de-escalate, defuse and harmonise difficulties that arise from the fears that drive conflicts. Promoting trust and lessening threat is by and large what principled negotiation aims for. The more we learn about negotiation, the more skilled we can be in bringing harmony into our lives. In time, ease in negotiating becomes second nature, spreading out in widening ripples beyond our own sphere of power. Here is how one couple made the shift to become better negotiators

Transforming conflict

As part of their overall separation negotiations, a couple – I will call them S and B - attempted to work on a 'fair share' approach, an agreed divide of spousal assets. Both had been in conflict for quite some time and each was feeling threatened. Understandably enough, because they had stopped co-operating, they had been focused only on self-preservation during the years when their marriage was failing. Naturally, when they arrived for mediation they found it extremely hard to co-operate in mutual and self-enhancing ways. Trust was low at the start of the process, so to begin with, I attempted to foster a climate of mutuality where the wisdom of finding a sustainable win-win solution that would honour the ongoing nature of their relationship as parents.

In principle, both agreed to this, it seemed to fit well with what each of them wanted, yet I was surprised when both arrived at the third session, with B saying things had changed. S, his partner, had for a number of years hidden a bank account that, by now, had accumulated substantial savings. S had built up funds by withholding a part of her salary and making regular contributions to an account solely in her own name. It emerged that B had stumbled on the account by chance and that an angry exchange had ensued. Now, revenging anger had set in. B had upped the ante by doing a bigger and more impacting deduction. Both reported that they were feeling miserable and in despair that they would ever find a solution. What felt worse to them was that their children were quite distraught, because they had inadvertently become embroiled in the escalating conflict. They each had the full support of their respective legal teams, who seemed to believe that resolution would be helped by a judicial decision. The stage was set for a court case. Equal and opposite righteousness would be put forward and ultimately a judgement would be reached.

Although decisions by a third party attempt to be fair, this usually involves the individuals giving up control over their decisions. Ultimately this was not what either wanted. However, all was not yet lost. S and B had at least returned for the third session. They could have cancelled.

I was surprised but not daunted; because it is precisely at such moments of crisis that I have seen couples turn the situation into an opportunity for positive change.

I suggested that it seemed to me that they each still had a bond of common concern for the worsening situation. Both acknowledged the consequences of disempowering themselves in the area of ongoing communication. Each had bought into a vision of positive parenting, where ongoing transparency and co-operation about their roles as parents would be essential. These points of concern and mutual interest would prove useful in staying the course of the mediation process. Both understood that while a third party might bring settlement, it would not compare to the benefits of learning to be empowered negotiators themselves.

To work things out, each of them now needed to take their power to negotiate the assurances, safety checks and co-operation they would need to create a fair and balanced agreement. It would involve an unravelling back to primal fears about needs. Both worried about scarcity and each felt at risk of going without because they perceived the other as not wanting to be fair. When they took to the idea of balancing needs they began to commit to the steps that would make it possible for each of them to have a fair share. Letting go of the short-sighted belief that one of them being left short would bring happiness and harmony was the insight that made change possible. Broader awareness of the fact that we are always affecting, and being affected by, life's own need for equilibrium points to the futility of short-sighted solutions.

With honest engagement S and B both played their part and got to the deeper essence of what lay behind their conflict; they found that fear of losing out was a significant factor. Each felt that the other would not look out for them in a fair manner. Talking through this, setting out criteria that would seem fair to each of them, was how they became creative and got to a win-win solution. Initially, they were business-like. Yet as they began to feel safer, trust returned and more respectful relating began. To the credit of each of them, this meant staying the course for six months; their heartfelt arguments on fears and hopes were exchanged over this time. After the usual initial difficulties that come about at the beginning of any conflict both engaged fully and came to be generous to one another. The healing was palpable and the consequence for their children immense. At the final session the children came to be part of the closing ritual. Both parents spoke to the children about how they would each be taking care of the ongoing family needs.

Although it is always sad to grieve the loss implicit in marital separation, healing comes more surely as the structures that ensure future living arrangements are well taken care of. For S and B, beyond their fear of losing out, both had found an ability to be decent with each other. There is always something very healing in witnessing a return of fairness. *It boded well for their future.*

THE ART OF EASING CONFLICT
20 CREATIVE TIPS TO EASE THE WAY

Here are some tips from the world of mediation that can help us move more sure-footedly in our negotiations:

1. Accept that you are entering a process in which you cannot absolutely know the outcome from the beginning.

2. Accept that you are co-creating the outcome.

3. Be aware that you are taking a first step and you may have to travel without any concrete evidence of trust. Trust begins as a seed; it needs time and conditions in order to grow – try taking a risk.

4. Make a specific agreement to put your fears, hostility or other emotional responses aside (even for a time). Commit to learning what the emotional response you are

experiencing is trying to teach you. Get to understand your emotions – improve on your emotional literacy. (You may need to talk this through with a genuine skilled person).

5. Ask for the safety assurances you need.

6. Commit yourself to persevering with the process – this includes remaining with the issue in hand. Acknowledge that a conflict which has oppressed over a long time may take time to resolve.

7. Develop options These include developing possibilities – creating a model of the *ideal*, thus freeing you to think about possibility (you can temper your idealism as you progress, if you need to); continue to dialogue where needs, concerns, wishes, hopes and fears are expressed in an open and honest way.

8. Have review breaks. Break to acknowledge progress; or take an overview. It will prevent fatigue.

9. Be aware of the intensity of your emotions. It is easy to "fly into a passion", as Shakespeare advised, but to apply the right amount, at the right time, to the right person, in the right situation is more a subtle art!

10. Actively concentrate on developing an attitude of patience and kindness. Check for a frozen heart. Temper your urgent desire to lash out to rid yourself of the conflict

11. Watch out for rigidity in your own or the other person's attitude. Rigidity usually indicates wounded trust – fear of losing face or loss of something more tangible.

12. Keep giving attention to your own sense of fairness. Get to understand it yourself so you can take responsibility for it, own it, communicate it, check it out and understand its consequence. This is the mark of maturity.

13. Actively listen to another's sense of fairness – question, check out and give feedback. Work to create mutuality.

14. Bring your own authority and power to the negotiations. Be autonomous. This doesn't rule out taking expert advice to help make an informed decision or asking for time to consider a matter. Both of these are healthy negotiation practices.

15. Put forward your own perception of 'truth' and listen for the other person's 'truth.' Understand that many 'truths' are values and have cultural meaning.

16. Understand the potency of different power bases. Be aware of power imbalances.

17. Move around issues within the conflict. Don't place all your energy on resolving one part. Approach it a bit like a jigsaw puzzle. Some pieces are easier to

find later when more movement has occurred. Some people do pie charts on issues - this will partialize and break down conflicts into manageable size, but always remember that issues, like life, are interdependent. Resentment from one unresolved issue will often find its way to another, or will tie up energy and compound the situation.

18. Nourish your physical well-being and your spirits. Keep supportive, positive resources available to you. Fatigue is the greatest enemy to ongoing fruitful negotiations. Overwhelming discouragement and despair can set in at negotiations when we are over-tired.

19. Consider what solving this conflict may mean. Imagine and state what a good outcome would be. (It could be a secondary gain from the conflict that is preventing a solution). Can you believe it will free up your energy to get on with a positive life? Many conflicts have secondary gains.

20. Try out different ideas – e.g. 'blue-sky,' brainstorm solutions. Above all, believe in the expansive creative power of the universe that we all share in.

Once more with feeling

We saw earlier that we must choose our attitudes - creativity or conflict. We saw, too, how conflict takes us into power struggle while creativity brings us to empowerment. By its very nature, conflict tends towards win-lose, to opposition where 'either or' thinking dominates. Creativity tends us towards 'yes and', to win-win. Inevitably, a win-lose attitude triggers fear, while a win-win attitude builds trust.

To negotiate in keeping with the spirit of creativity we hold an attitude that lets us value others as well as ourselves; in doing so we can transform a win-lose attitude to a more win-win collaborative spirit.

To live is to journey - to collaborate is to work together on that journey. Commitment to mutuality is a vital way to live and one that brings hope to even the most entrenched conflicts. Yet it would be foolish to minimise the power of the emotional charge of conflict. Getting emotional clarity is perhaps the transformative step in easing conflict because difficulty with emotions cloud judgement and trap creative energy.

Emotional clearing

Most of us have days where we reach the end of our patience, our attention wanders and 'hopeful' is the last word to describe us. On such days we may feel rejected - and rejecting. Explanations may run dry, a crises occurs or a major transition brings on a loss that must be handled. We may be working too hard, expecting too much of ourselves or suffering from a lack of support and not saying 'no' to situations that are overwhelming. The list is infinite. However, with practice, we learn to unravel the lesson and to move through these times. We learn to have a more conscious encounter with our behaviour, thoughts and feelings so that we can categorise, clarify and bring some caring support to the issues on hand.

Leaving reactive habits behind

To be creative and bring ease to our situation, we are asked to move out of the habitual emotional ruts that trap us in conflict - to gain an understanding of what triggers the fear that leads there. We are asked to search for ways to co-operate so that we can build trust and release the vast untapped creative resources available in life.

Where emotions are understood, both trust and fear can be employed wisely. In this way we can live genuine lives, where we learn to consciously negotiate, resolve and make creative choices in our own particular sphere of influence. When we can tune in and ask what is going on with our emotions, ultimately we can live more humanely. Given the choice then, how can we get better at choosing to be creative rather that mire ourselves in conflict? A more conscious encounter with our reactive tendencies to fight and flight, and the attendant emotions that surround each, might just be the thing we need. Let us see now how our emotional landscape can be more user-friendly.

CHAPTER 12
NAVIGATING THE EMOTIONAL
LANDSCAPE

Emotional literacy

In his book *Emotional Intelligence* Daniel Goleman draws the attention to the importance of learning more about our emotional impulses. He quotes from Frances Moore Lappe's *The Art of Democracy,* in which she wrote that managing emotional impulses has social benefits. "It opens the way to empathy, to real listening, to taking another person's perspective." Empathy, says Goleman, leads to caring, altruism and compassion. "Seeing things from another's perspective breaks down biased stereotypes, and so, breeds tolerance and acceptance of differences. These capacities are ever more called on in our increasingly pluralistic society, allowing people to live together in mutual respect and creating the possibility of productive public discourse. These are the basic arts of democracy."

That said, in reality we all need help to understand the complex world of emotion.

It sometimes can require care and the utmost patience to decode the range of emotions that permeate our day-to-day negotiations.

Emotions matter

In all life's encounters, arousal of emotion is central. As humans we have a wide emotional range that can affect whether or not outcomes are creative. Our health and well-being, and consequently our creative energy, is deeply affected by our ability to deal with our emotions. Vitality is determined by how clear we are about our emotional responses. Awareness of our impulses and an ability to literally read into their meaning transforms them from foe to friend. It is this literacy that helps keep emotions from stagnating, festering and becoming toxic.

As we learn to understand our emotions we no longer are bound by them but can investigate what they are telling us. We can then choose how to respond appropriately.

When we can truly experience emotions, integrate, respond and explore them consciously, we are free to express in ways that enrich our communications.

Understanding emotions will mean we can modulate and experience them. In modulating we can read them, check out what they mean. This can guide us in our actions and perceptions. Nothing is more helpful in negotiations with conflict than having emotional literacy. When we become fluent we can negotiate well, enjoying life and navigating the rough patches that are an inevitable part of living out our truest potential.

Destructive fights

The primal response in the face of threat is deep. Healthy fear is a sensory response to danger and, as such, it is vital to our safety. Our bodies respond to signals of fear by releasing adrenalin that gives us an energy boost for action. In this way, fear is useful and necessary.

Chronic fear, though, is not useful; it is dangerous to health. It keeps us in a state of high alert causing our blood pressure to stay high for too long. In a state of chronic fear our discernment becomes flawed and we operate in a state of generalized anxiety. We can find it hard to make good judgements. Deep feelings of hopelessness can flood day-to-day activities and, over time, anxiety can turn to depression. Untreated or uninterrupted, depression can colour our view of life and lead to, at best, stagnation and rigidity - at worst, despair. Understanding emotions will begin to empower; it will build trust. Earlier we saw that trust and fear are key elements in creativity and conflict. Trust will empower us with love and the spirit of creativity while fears can fuel the hatred that provokes conflict

Fear-fuelled hatred ... trust-empowered love

Love and fear, it is said, are our core emotions, although we most often talk of love and hate. Much of what becomes our day-to-day run of the mill emotional range can usually be unravelled back to one of these primal drives. The heart, an international symbol of love, has always been seen to play a strong part in making helpful change. Bringing heart and head to our conflicts will, as we have seen, bring benefits in time. In the healing professions we talk about *encouragement,* of giving heart or of having the heart for something. Love is experienced as an emotion that warms us and opens our eyes to beauty. In all walks of life love is much sought and true love is enduringly tended.

Today, many people speak about the resonance of emotions. That love is an upbeat, high vibration emotion, is generally undisputed. Love is the master trust-builder. We know its power as we experience it. Falling in love can let us scale mountains.

When we are unafraid, love can shine through, creativity flourishes and trust builds. Hatred can be viewed as a primal response that helps generate the energy needed to oust or be rid of a threat to our wellbeing. We will often fight to our own detriment in the face of real or perceived threat. Many of us have had little experience of learning to read our emotional impulses. Education about emotions can be trial and error in most people's lives. Yet when we can learn to be clear about emotions we have the foundations for healthy negotiations. By learning what lies behind the positions we take in conflict, we start to negotiate in more humanitarian ways.

Learning that, when conscious, all emotions are essentially healthy will be an enormous step forward to easing conflict.

Unconscious fight and flight response: the dangers

Such is the power of 'fight and flight' reactions in our daily lives that to be unaware is to make the world less safe. Unconscious fears can exacerbate tension in any situation. Real or perceived fears about our needs can trigger feelings of threat, put us into conflict and block our creativity. Much of what we see in the form of conflict is driven by real and perceived troubles with emotions between ourselves and others

Emotions that flow from fear quite literally flood the arena, causing both head and heart ache. Negotiating our conflicts is always dynamic. In practising the art of easing conflict we need to keep a caring focus on solutions, taking time to unravel what lies behind the conflict. Behaviours can run the full gamut of struggle, manipulation, cop-out and drop-out - sometimes banishing all hope for consensus building or fair play. Yet it is only when we get stuck in habitual, persistent and unconscious patterns of fear that we are in danger of being mired in conflict.

Healthy fears

Fear, as we have seen, can alert us to the need for healthy assertion or withdrawal. Yet, when unrelieved over time, it can tip us into toxic patterns that run a spectrum from depression through to aggression.

At the deepest strata, fear instincts that are healthy will alert us to set boundaries. Yet these alerts may be in need of attention. Habitual red alert systems may be in need of an overhaul. We may be held back from easing conflicts and finding pathways to real progress because of unchecked fear. We may hunker down and close off our creative spirit because we have not yet built the levels of trust that will promote resolve of problems through creative negotiation. Deep down below the surfaces of conflict lies fear of loss, the loss of something we deem important. It may be loss of dignity, loss of the resources we need to live, loss of security, loss of empowerment or loss of one's right to inclusion; it is the awareness and understanding of our fear and how we choose our responses that requires attention.

Because fear triggers fight and flight responses, we can, without being aware of it, get stuck in extremes of these two modes. At one extreme our feelings and behaviours may tip us into passivity; at the other extreme, into aggression. Acting from an extreme of fear, we may respond to our legitimate needs in an excessive fashion. We may attack, or we may give up passively, accepting that no change is possible. If we are stuck in *flight* mode, we may be prone to victimization; stuck in *fight* mode, we may have a tendency to lunge forward and be abusive. Without awareness of how the mechanisms of fear operate, primal alarm bells calling us to fight or flight can cause us to see-saw between avoidance and hostility. The problem with this is that it can push us to habitual extremes and diminish our healthy instinctual ability to sense and respond appropriately.

In every negotiation, as noted earlier, we need to know when to withdraw or when to act assertively. Denial of fear can become pervasive, so it hinders rather than helps, while fear that is conscious acts as a radar to help us move wisely.

Primal fear reactions

In *flight* we are being given the cue to withdraw, to stand back. In *fight* we are being aroused to move into action.

Primal response is very concerned with life and death so the voltage from it may need a little civilizing. These primal reactions are old brain responses and have our survival at heart; they hold the philosophy that life is about survival of the fittest - it's a jungle out there!

Let's look at what happens when what we perceive as threatening sends a signal to our primal being.

Unconscious *fight* path

<u>FIGHT</u>
LEADS TO POWER STRUGGLE,
OPPOSITION & FORCE

In unconscious fight mode, as aggression escalates, desperate efforts are made to be rid of the threat that frightens us. Our objects of fear, of course, are often real or imagined, yet it will bring into being the hatred that sets the scene for riddance. In fight we may re-actively attack head-on, blustering and dominating as we go. We might act from undue force that will spark dissonance and fuel conflict.

Domination, subjugation or annihilation can become a prevailing and governing pattern where hatred operates without being checked out. It is a short hop to downright destruction.

Unconscious *flight* path

<u>FLIGHT</u>
LEADS TO DENIAL, AVOIDANCE &
APPEASEMENT

In unconscious *flight,* we will refuse, deny, appease. We may stagnate and shut down. In this extreme, passivity can become habitual. As passive participants, we may freeze, wear armour camouflage and hide out. Staying put and making little effort to live vitally, we may become depressed, resentful or ill with frustration. We may replace assertive, healthy withdrawal with minimising, appeasing and camouflaging. In *flight* we may eventually become indifferent, despair, unable or unwilling to encounter the realities of the conflict we face. When such fear responses become patterns they disrupt trust. Rebuilding trust and diffusing toxic fear can take a long time.

Toxic fears

Fear can lead to inflexibility and to maladaptive thoughts, feelings and behaviours. Over time, with repetition and habit, these can harden into patterns that take their toll on our spirits. When *flight* becomes our habitual unconscious response, we may become overly passive. Turned in, fear can dim our life force and cause serious wastage of creative potential. Fear alert may be habitual and misleading. Unexplored, it can make us under-functional or ill.

When *fight* becomes our habitual response, fear metamorphoses into feelings of rage, belligerence and cynicism. When the high voltage of fear response is turned out, it can hurt others. Not surprisingly, these responses put us out of balance, causing strong compensatory defences that interrupt the flow of creativity.

Duration and intensity

Our levels of arousal in conflict create biological responses; highly charged emotions affect the basics of health. As noted, heart rate and blood pressure can become pathologically affected by prolonged distress. Fear that permeates conflict may frustrate our capacity for love and work, create a self-fulfilling prophecy and leave us feeling unloved or disempowered. These become the very conditions necessary for conflict to thrive. Conflicts around the world are fuelled by fear that sets the scene for fight or flight and makes for frightened people. When fears block they create densi-ties that get in the way of the transparency needed for honest dialogue, destroying the trust we need for the wellspring of creativity to surge.

To manage our conflicts we need to have the abil-ity to understand, own and integrate the emotions that tag along with fear. Absence of fear is not possible, yet building trust is. Creativity involves mastery over the re-active power of toxic fear and the implementation of the things that can proactively build trust.

It can require care and patience to de-escalate the high arousal that primal fear can send out.

De-escalating conflict

De-escalating conflict asks us to separate the person from the problem and to move into a way of relat-ing that works for creative win-win solutions. Healthy fear, as we have seen, will alert us to assert or yield as needed, but fear can also complicate and be problem-atic when it becomes a pattern.

Lack of awareness of how our emotions colour our negotiation style can sabotage success. Overwhelm will stop negotiation in its track. An experienced mediator knows that de-escalating, decoding and releasing emo-tions in a balanced and congruent way is central to easing conflict. Many negotiations end when emotions flood the arena where talks are taking place. Patterns that flow from toxic fears have a knock-on effect for all living systems.

Decoding emotions

Recognising and decoding the burdensome thinking, feeling and behaviour that come via fear is sometimes difficult. Fear is often encoded deeply in other emotions - when we seem most unable to resolve conflict. In embracing our fears and not running away, we get to come to terms with how fear can help us navigate creatively. We can also see how it can hold us back, when it harmfully drives us to outbursts that fuel conflict.

Acceptance is a first step. Acceptance does not necessarily mean we will like, or endorse, events; neither does it mean that we remain a passive bystander to the issue at hand. Ease in conflict is always preceded by understanding of the reality that we need to negotiate some duality. Conflict within ourselves can overflow to the circumstances around us, amplifying emotions - either consciously by the impressions we give directly, or unconsciously by the impressions we give off. Emotions are part of everyone's story. Becoming skilled at decoding our emotions in the personal sphere can have real and sustainable benefits in the wider circles of our lives.

When we can decode emotions in a healthy and timely way, we will have the opportunity to build the kind of trust that lets each of us unfurl our full creative potential. But when we are *not* emotionally aware, it can have us act in less than creative ways. These can culminate in the kind of thinking, behaviour and feeling patterns that move us out of the sphere of creative living and keep us stuck in ongoing spirals of conflict. In turn these lead to further knock- on cycles of anger.

The knock-on effects of fear

We each manifest our own unique emotional response to fears as they arise; we each have antennae that can, when in good shape, guide us wisely. When we get locked into fight or flight responses that keep us angry, we can benefit greatly by having some perspective on how anger can be managed. Knowing how anger can help or hinder, knowing its shape and form, we will not tend to hold it unconsciously.

Instead we will learn more about managing the anger that naturally arises to protect us, and see how to recognise the danger when it gets complicated. Being clear about anger will help us to get on with what it takes to to stay creative and let go of conflict.

CHAPTER 13
ANGER MANAGEMENT

Becoming a player

As we develop a willingness to show up with heart and head and deal with our problems, we can move off blame and begin to focus on a new future. Focusing on who was right or wrong, who is at fault, who started the problem, will miss the real point - genuine ease will only come about as we commit to negotiate with our heart and head engaged. Attention to this principle will keep us moving step-by-step to build toward a more creatively empowered way of living. We may need to learn assertiveness and yielding rather than aggression and capitulation. We may need to become more accountable rather than feeling guilty. We may need to let go and move on rather than stay put resentfully. As we aim for personal creative empowerment we will realise that we need to handle the disempowering patterns that keep us in conflict.

As we have seen in negotiation this will mean naming our needs. It will also mean that we must understand what lies within the feelings we experience. When we can do both we will find that, beyond the bubbling surface of conflict that fuels cyclical hatred and a desire for revenge and counter-revenge, there is a legitimate issue in need of discussion. Feeling depressed or belligerent during negotiations will require us to delve deeper to find out what imperatives we are operating within. Many forms of negotiation are sabotaged because we cannot handle the feelings involved. The fire of anger, for example, can burn, smoulder and spoil the chance of creative connections.

Responsibility

Responsibility will ask that we 'own' our thoughts, behaviours and emotions and take responsibility for them, accepting them as our teachers, finding what lies behind them

It will ask us to become more attuned to our capacity for change - to be responsible for the choices we make and the consequences they trigger. And it will ask us to hold that the point of power for change and resolution is always with us.

It can be easy to project or dismiss our thoughts, emotions and behaviours, blaming others and learning nothing from them. Understanding emotions will get us started. Acknowledging ownership and taking responsibility for it is how we empower ourselves to move into our creativity and bring ease to conflict.

Approaching anger

Anger is a healthy emotion when used wisely. It has healing, invigorating properties that move us to improve situations. Validating anger as a normal healthy response is often a first step in releasing the information it holds.

Anger is also a very dangerous emotion so it must be partnered responsibly. We have seen how, when in free flow, it can disrupt rationality and so intimidate people. In difficult conflict situations anger has usually become complicated so that it has splintered-off in many directions. Anger can show in differing guises so recognising what these are can help us understand them - greasing the wheels of movement, change and possibility.

For instance, shame and guilt often join forces with belligerence, producing very tough, resistant, resentful and destructive patterns. These mindsets will sabotage negotiations just as readily as belligerence because all of them can make dialogue difficult. Unravelling these compounded feelings will help us get in touch with anger that is part of a healthy emotional repertoire, one that may well prove useful to learning more about the issue at hand.

The value of anger

Healthy anger arises because we perceive that a person or situation threatens to violate us in some way. We need to hear our anger, feel it and understand where it is coming from. Speaking about it may be the first step but, more importantly, we need to *feel* it and trace it back to where the hurt or violation has arisen.

When anger is not felt, integrated and expressed appropriately, it can easily turn to aggression (active or passive). Aspects of anger can be energising - venting, acting out and dumping are all common responses which can help people feel in charge. But they are not, in fact, helpful.

Research on anger demonstrates that it is helpful to feel one's anger and it is helpful to articulate the feelings and issues around the anger, but it is not helpful to lash out.

Venting anger, that is speaking about it in ways that keep us angry, without consciously connecting to the feelings, can pump up emotional arousal, leaving people angrier. Suppressing anger is not good but suppressing the repetitive raging about it is beneficial. In this way we can take responsibility for finding out what lies behind it and move to work it out.

Take, for example, a couple I will call J and T.

Aggressive belligerence had become their behavioural and emotional habit.

They were grandparents when they came to mediation. When their children had grown and left home, they had physically built a dividing wall in their family home. But even the wall did not prevent abusive incursions by both. The police and the courts had told them that they did not want to hear from them again until they had taken responsibility for sorting out their fights. To add insult to injury, they had been told at one court hearing that they were wasting time. To be fair to the justice system it *was* a waste of everyone's time if all that was on offer was punishment and counter-punishment. Neither T nor J could understand the negative attachment each had to their fight. With years of abusive fighting behind them, both had emotional, spiritual and physical scars.

The healing process for T and J

As the healing task is one of personal growth, both T and J were now being asked to discuss a very painful subject - how trust and fear about safety were operating in their lives. No prizes for guessing that this rotten pattern had lingered since childhood. Both had been beaten severely as children, because this was the currency their families had used to 'settle' issues. They learned to suppress normal anger, while their parents vented their own in terrible outbursts. Where feelings go unexpressed in healthy ways, children often learn that they should not be angry. Going from emotions into action without any thought can be very troublesome. Acting unconsciously on emotions by and large will not help or heal - but may give relief for a short time. Often intense rage in the present will stem from a legacy of pain or hurt that belongs in the past. Or it may compound into a pattern that is passed on generation after generation. This was what had happened for T and J. The toxic anger that spurred their hateful rage had spanned three generations.

Both were now in poor health. They were battle weary. T and J were now looking for some peace in their lives. They had been angry long enough, they were amenable to try something else.

T and J worked within the process of mediation for some time and came up with a plan. They agreed not to encroach on each other's physical or psychological space and to be respectful in their communications and actions. They acknowledged that they were both raw and edgy in relation to each other and that all arrangements that might be needed to safeguard ongoing mutual relationships with their grown children and grandchildren would be made with notice and with formal businesslike arrangements. This set up boundaries that they each accepted. I knew their wounds ran deep and that they were both sorry, but neither could say it. Forgiveness takes time.

However, do you know what? They cried in relief on the day they read their final separation agreement. A year on, at their review, they had two jointly-attended family occasions behind them and had both managed to keep to the terms they agreed. Now somewhat stronger, they said sorry to each other. In wishing them peace in their retirement, I couldn't help thinking that the school of hard knocks had handed out a very harsh lesson to these highly engaging grandparents.

Conditioning

How we think, feel and behave is developed generally in response to the experiences that condition us. To have a more conscious encounter with our behaviour, thoughts or feelings will help clarify where we are coming from. Negotiating, exercising choice and living pro-actively will all be easier as we get more switched on to what makes us tick. Living reactively is not living from creative empowerment. We give up choice when we are reactive. The more self-aware we are, the sooner we can begin to heal and grow into our fullest potential. Separating out the behaviour, thoughts and feelings that help us from those that hold us back is a very empowering process. More than anything, it will help lessen the type of reactivity that leads to aggression.

The harsh reality of aggression

Aggressive attacks will hit out to hurt the emotional, spiritual or physical well-being of ourselves and others, either directly or indirectly. Aggressive abuse can target a person, a group or even a nation; suffice to say that, because we are essentially interconnected to one another, the effects of aggression ripple out to all of us. Voltage can run the full gamut from high to low, with levels of belligerence varying in destructiveness.

Anger management has become part of coaching curricula in the worlds of sport, business and education.

Asserting a boundary may involve physical, emotional or psychological boundaries that let the cycle of abuse and counter-abuse abate. Moving off the 'power over' mentality is the spirit that will make real change. However, even though having a boundary that allows for disengagement from abusive cycles of behaviour is essential, getting past toxic habits may require something more. Writer and psychologist Tony Humphreys suggests that, even where abuse is stopped by 'whistle-blowers' and a boundary asserted, it "does not deal with the issues of insecurity and poor regard for self and others." It is within the relationship with oneself and between self and others that matters are improved.

Where deep wounds exist, it is important that we find someone who can help get to the primary wound site, where much of the voltage lies. Moving on may require an acknowledgement or an apology from the person or people involved to help heal such wounding - failing that, an acceptance that allows one to draw a line in the sand and let go of engagement in an abusive cycle. Sometimes this naturally occurs through the lessons of day-to-day living; at other times, deeper attention is required. Making amends in a ritual or symbolic gesture may help in some situations too, but it is when we become accountable that we are taken out of shame and into empowerment.

Accountability versus shame

Guilt and shame are often connected. Shame is seldom consciously acknowledged or articulated - it is a state of feeling that is almost inadmissible. Often we report guilt rather than shame. There is something so frightening about shame that people will express a great range of responses but stop short of experiencing the feeling of shame. Shame breeds more shame. It arises when someone is told, directly or indirectly, that they are not good enough, deficient and not deserving or valued. When someone feels shame, particularly when it is held unconsciously, there is a real danger that they will attempt to be rid of these feelings in a maladaptive way - for example, by shaming others or developing symptoms that either mask or worsen their sense of shame. Seeking power over others by demeaning is an end game of shame.

When someone is fairly sturdy, shame is not experienced as all-pervasive but is linked to a particular issue. More like embarrassment or what is known in restorative justice as an 'integrative shame'; it is linked to the issue on hand, perhaps behaviour. It does not demean the person and acknowledges that we are intrinsically more than behaviour alone. Linked to behaviour we can name it, feel it, learn from it and then make an adjustment. When we can dust ourselves off and move on we will avoid complications.

Accountability is about taking appropriate steps to make changes, but guilt as an emotion is harrowing. Unlike taking appropriate responsibility for our behaviour and making amends, guilt involves a generalized and consistent feeling that can take hold and spoil relationships. Guilt blocks real dialogue and will often involve taking all the responsibility for a difficulty. This has obvious pitfalls, not least a feeling of overwhelm that, in turn, can lead to poor assessment and trigger short-sighted responses. 'Name and blame' policies often feed spurious interest where little is learned. When shame becomes fixed, however, it acquires an absolute quality. Worst of all, it can accumulate and becomes contagious. Those who shame have usually had it passed on to them. Resentments build up when shame is left unchecked, complicating access to living more fully in tune with our creative centre.

Resentment versus letting go

It is sometimes said that resentment is hardened anger; anger that has not seen the light of day. When anger is 'underground,' it becomes fixed, causing it to stagnate at the point where the hurt first occurred. Hardened anger leads to a build-up of resentment, resistance and hostility, to name some of the difficult complications. When we feel resentful we can easily slip into a role of victim or abuser and strike a blow at our creative empowerment. Resistance is indirect and characterised by a lack of acknowledgement that keeps us from being a player. Such behavioural habits can cross generations and, although intensity of feeling may be linked to a long-gone original hurt, the refusnik in us may now have little conscious connection with it.

Loss and fear of loss is at epidemic proportions in today's world. Many people struggle with internalized angers that are so far removed from the source of the original anger that they cannot see the necessity of giving any time or attention to it.

Low-grade resentment can often permeate groups small and large. Resentment that is held chronically is hard to get at. It can be played out as resistance and this, along with denying and withholding in a relationship can be very unproductive in negotiating conflict. While resistance can be seen as a passive attempt at self-protection, it can lead to cut-offs - a refusal to play, which can be very destructive in negotiation. With cut-off the flow of energy is lost, so creative communication is more likely to break down.

Resistance differs from letting go. The latter is a behaviour that is healthy because it is conscious and overt. Letting go will usually only happen when we consciously acknowledge the anger and deal with it fairly; it may involve grieving a loss so that we make room for new beginnings. Loss is part of the cycle of life; acknowledging it makes space for the 'new' to enter. In the East 'completion' is the term used to acknowledge the end of one thing and mark the beginning of another. It normalises change so that we can consciously deal with it. Cycles are part of life, in the comings and goings when something has run its course and has been dealt with in as complete a way as is possible in a given time or place.

Forgiveness is essentially a form of letting go, a decision not to be blocked by the debris of trapped emotion.

Feeling angry all the time may be a way of putting off facing up to a real loss that is in need of grieving. For some, being angry is better than being sad. When we by-pass the sadness that is an inherent part of the cycles of life we may postpone the acceptance that allows a creative renewal to surge; we may stay in a fog of denial.

Acceptance versus denial

Acceptance asks only that we move out of the tendency to avoid issues or to force unnatural change - because, when we use either avoidance or force we will decrease the chance of timely resolve. Resolve asks that we first accept what is. Acceptance creates a space where we can start to frame and contain our hopes, fears and goals. When we act from fear we behave and respond very differently than when we are hopeful. Working things out in a way that brings ease to conflict can mean getting mutuality or a graceful completion that brings closure and a new beginning. We may need to learn to ask for our needs, and ask again; to ask differently, to show gratitude - and expect to get at least some of what we ask for. We may need to be ready to give way and let another have what *they* need. The complexity of being human in a constantly changing environment requires us to move out of any tendency to live in the trance of flight, or the spin of fight. We need to understand just how much power these common emotions bring to our day-to-day challenges. Whether this power is consciously understood is up to us.

Emotional understanding

As with most things, degree matters. When it comes to common everyday emotional responses, in fact, it is the degree and duration to which we repress emotions that brings complications.

It is by knowing the meaning and power of these responses that we become more emotionally literate and can stop them hardening to destructive levels. Huge difficulty arises when we internalise the negative emotional states, as they limit the possibility for reaching our natural creative potential.

Yet each one of us can learn to handle our emotions. The heart and head approach to negotiating conflict will bring progress in time. Certainly, when we connect at a 'feeling' level and place the principles of fairness centre stage, we begin the process of change. When we become willing to move through the complicated fears, angers and suspicions that block us, we can bring all our faculties to bear on problem solving. Moving on will be done at our own pace, in our own time.

Our own pace

Change, as we have seen, is a constant process; it is the only certainty. Progress is up to us. In real terms this allows us to see 'possibility' as something we can believe in and hold on to. If we were not changing, dynamic and evolving beings, progress would be impossible.

Staying in process will bring resolve in a step-by-step way. Healing will ask that we release the old hurts that keep our best at bay. It will ask that we release fixed ideas that create obstacles in our lives. Little by little, moving progressively, changes will occur. We can start with more awareness of our approach to dealing with the issues at hand. In this way we can ease our conflicts. As we have seen earlier, unresolved issues have a habit of recurring. We can view this as a total nuisance or we can see it as an elegant fact of nature - teaching us that we may need to make a new approach. Sometimes as something resurfaces in our life, it gives us a chance to look at it afresh and to interegate it and sort it out more thoroughly. Once we buy into the truth that at the core of each us, there is a power surge of creativity, connected and inter-connected in the wider collective, we will feel less daunted. When we realise that we can mobilize our energy to face the issues at hand, we will find it easier to make changes.

Making progress

As we have seen, inner and outer landscapes matter when it comes to easing conflict, so change is usually brought by the interplay of both. We differ in our levels of readiness to change, in our circumstance and our hopes. We differ in our histories too. Loss, as we have seen, is part of everyone's life, yet some people will have more to grieve than others. The consequence of destructive conflict will require painstaking attention in order to process the changes needed for new shoots of renewal to push through. The impact of conflict differs from situation to situation. Compound conflicts may need specific and careful handling. Because conflict can be difficult, being able to call on someone can help a lot. Caring support can help us to navigate the issues in a gradual process. Support can soothe the way.

Engaging skilled help

As outlined in Part 2, it may be good to call on skilled help to get past our blocks, that said; it is developing a willingness to make a start on easing conflict that will set us on our way.

Skilled interventions can offer inputs that will help us to be more emotionally literate. Importantly, therapeutic help can model and teach emotional literacy, helping us to become more willing and capable of exploring our emotions. By pacing our process, a skilled helper can partialize problems to manageable size and prevent over-whelm - thus promoting perseverance. Skilled input also helps us to stay with issues and to plan change.

A skilled helper can input information and support healthy change by spotting, referencing and pacing our readiness for change. We can indeed be helped - but we, too, must play our part.

CHAPTER 14
HOPE FOR THE FUTURE

Pathfinders

Gail Sheehy is the author of *Pathfinders*, a book about how creative people find paths through situations - people who cultivate in some way the concentrated optimism to get around obstacles. "Pathfinders," she writes, "are made, not born" and adds that these people are "just as concerned with their inner achievements as they are with outer attainments." Sheehy tells how, when researching her book, she interviewed Trappist monks. 'I told them that I was looking for people who show virtuosity in handling change in the turning points of life.' A stricken look crossed the faces I could see. 'Virtuosity,' the abbot stammered, 'is a very difficult word for us ...I explained that by virtuosity I meant creativity, in the sense of the creative task of existence. The abbot was visibly relieved. 'Oh, he said, I was afraid you meant goodness!' ..."

Sheehy adds that selflessness was not part of even a monk's lifestyle. The monks' view, she found, supported her research and alerted her to one important criterion for the pathfinder; they would not be involved exclusively in "doing their own thing or solely in caring for others, but in seeking to balance both".

Nowhere more than in our negotiations with conflict will the importance of 'self and other' play out. Naturally arising differences can easily create a gap between our reality and our expectations. Good negotiations as we have seen will generally involve an artful interplay with both self and other; this includes the reality and expectation of each. All productive negotiation has us straddle the real with the possible; we must engage in combining reality checks with the 'blue-skying' of new possibility. As we have seen too, differences offer a wide spectrum of variation that will invite us to get more practised in handling it.

It is easy to see how endurance, perseverance and fairness will be required to bring the harmony that lets us work things out together. On the creative path we will be asked to negotiate around obstacles, reconcile mismatch and broaden our views to allow for differing perspectives. When we hold hope for inclusiveness, we will continue to bring gradual shifts in individual consciousness in this ever evolving world. To remain discerning, meeting challenges afresh, honours creativity. In the evolutionary nature of things we can learn to be more flexible. Creativity is often said to mean rule-breaking, alternative and likely to be the domain of the few. It does indeed ask us to move off fixed rules, certainties and petrified conformity towards openness, exploration and innovation.

Yet to be creative in a sustainable and renewable way will ask us to make choices, to break new ground, while not losing sight of our common humanity. *Fixed thinking is the death of creativity.*

In being creative we embrace and learn from a wide variety of sources. We welcome them all as an impetus for stimulation and expansion, for change and growth, for surprise and novelty; in a word, for creativity. It is in the connection and understanding that creativity is an innate part of each of us that possibility for hope resides; with hope in attendance we can begin to build trust. Maturity asks us to move off stereotyping, generalizing and narrowing our perspectives. Living with a creative spirit is healthy; it will ask us to explore, question, experiment, play and discover. It will ask that we take a risk as we support, include and respect the expressions of others. Risk will mean we will make mistakes, trust when we should not and *vice versa*. Yet, getting past these times is what makes us stress-hardy.

When we accept that diversity is a given and a part of our blueprint, we quickly get used to the idea that we are all interconnected, that what comes around, goes around. If we sacrifice the possibility of a broad view of difference, we may become fragmented and may make short-sighted decisions - decreasing our creative connectivity. As we embrace the spirit of globalization we will require a more expansive viewfinder.

The global village

In these times of rapid change, we are attempting to embrace the notion of living in a global village - a concept that is yet to attain real familiarity. How can we get along? What are our challenges? What do we need?

We now communicate in ways that were not available to previous generations. By providing ourselves with the know-how and experiences that help us feel both grounded yet fully switched on, we can fine-tune what we need to meet the challenges of the 21st century in a more creative way

We have so much cumulative technology, information and experience in today's world that trust in our ability to work together, to problem-solve, can both potentially and realistically be very high. The Internet can give us instant connection to one another. We have worldwide relationship networks that can be strengthened and harnessed to build the trust that unleashes creativity. When we begin to understand that sustainable creativity will only flourish where trust is present we will take more seriously our common task of long-haul trust building. Building trust is done in the day-to-day relationships of our lives.

Long-haul trust building

The capacity to build trust goes to the heart of making peace with conflict. Trust is not fixed, but involves us in a 'dance' of holding on and letting go as we manage and weave the transitions of living. Trust levels wax and wane in the lives of all of us because we are dynamic and subject to flux and change. Fairness, as we have seen, is central in maintaining ongoing creativity and is always being reckoned, either consciously or unconsciously, in our negotiations.

Yet it is reasonable to ask, how can we cultivate trust in these complex times that have been dubbed the 'age of anxiety'? How often have we said, "I do believe in a better way, but things are hard to change." It is true we see rotten patterns being repeated; war and recovery seem to be a futile cycles that frustrate genuine progress.

However as we gradually change at a personal level, so that trust-building becomes a part of us, we can gradually imbue it to our institutions. Johann Wolfgang von Goethe advises: "As soon as you trust yourself and you will know how to live."

In today's world the call to creativity is a call to trust-building. Initiatives to build trust engage the energy of millions of individuals around the world - keeping a focus on the trust that releases creativity, staying encouraged, will open doors to possibility. It will sustain the ideology that can breed optimism for powerful change.

Paradoxically, if we wait until we have *perfect* trust, we may wait forever.

Why there is reason for hope

Today's realism was often inspired by yesterday's ideal. Realists are good with *the 'nuts and bolts'* of things. Idealists are good for *'visions'*. Both working well together, respecting and valuing the merit of each other's energy, can create great synergy. Global consciousness is made up of the totality of the people of the world. Because institutions are formed by a collective of individuals, change is gradually implemented by individuals. Trust-building in institutions might ask that we slow down and negotiate from a spirit of empowerment. Speed is a worry when negotiating because the dialogue, change and structures that build trust take time, especially where problems have a long, deep history. Some may protest, " How can we go around negotiating with everyone all the time, we'd get nothing done!" Yet, in settings where trust is promoted by building consensus, more lasting changes take hold and any tendency to bully can be dissipated. Increasing this spirit may be just what it takes to prevent the blockages and blusters of conflicts. A faster culture may think it will increase efficiency; yet people are not machines - they are individuals with reciprocal and essential relationships to each other. If we dishonour this we may lose out on our sense of connection, Sociologist McKenzie Wark's quip, "We no longer have roots, we have aerials." says something about the disorientation of fast-changing modern life. We need both roots and aerials if we are to fashion structures that transmit the creativity to ease conflict.

Writing as a nonagenarian, the American author-historian Studs Terkel suggests with the title of his book that *Hope Dies Last*. Hope among groups, he tells us, surges up from the grass roots; hope does not operate top down. Of course, leaders can encourage and those with experience can help, yet hope for change must spring afresh in each one of us. My book has been about easing conflict, about tapping into our innate creativity. It has aimed to look at how our fears fuel conflict and how building trust can help creativity. It aims to encourage creativity because in doing so we can ease conflict. When we overlook the power of the small effort, we may be unravelling the core fabric that underpins our world. Sabotage of bigger efforts later on may be caused by forgetting the need for harmony at a personal level.

The world, it seems, will change one person at a time and, as always, new beginnings start in very small ways.

Essentially, to ease conflict we have to understand that we are all governed by the universal principles that interconnect us in the vast, awesome and creative moving picture of life.

There is indeed reason for hope. Consciousness shifts are happening all around us and the more we can embrace them, the more we will have the foundations for a healthy way of living. The small steps to peace-making begin with ourselves and ripple out in widening circles. Inevitably this will nourish creativity.

KEY SOURCES AND FURTHER READING

Bach, E. (1998)*The Twelve Healers And Other Remedies*.
Ohio;Mc Graw Hill

Bateson, G. (1972), *Steps to an Ecology of Mind*. New York:
Ballantine

Beckett, S. (1984) *Worstward*. London; Calder Publications

Benjamin, R. (1990) *"The Physics of Mediation; Reflections
on Scientific Theory in Professional Practice"* Mediation
Quarterly, Volume8, Number 2

Boldt, L. G. (1999) *The Tao of Abundance*, London: Penguin

Bowlby, J. (1969,1973, 1980) *Attachment and Loss,* Vols1, 2,
3. London: Hogarth Press

Browne Walker,B.(1992) *I Ching Book or Changes*. New
York;St.Martin's Griffen,

Bruner, J. (1974) *Beyond the Information Given*. London:
Allen & Unwin Ltd

Csikszentmihalyi, M.(1996) *Creativity; Flow and the
Psychology of Discovery and Invention*. New York; Harper
Collins

Capra, F. (1997) *The Web of Life*. New York: Doubleday

Crum, T. (1987) *The Magic of Conflict*. New York: Simon &
Schuster

Chopra, D. (1989) *Quantum Healing*. New York: Bantam
Books

Chopra, D. (2005) *Synchro Destiny* London; Random House

De Chardin, T. (1964) *The Future of Man*. New York: Harper
& Row

Dickinson, E. (1955) *The Complete Poems* Boston; Little
Brown

Erikson, E. H. (1964) *Childhood and Society* New York;
W.W, Norton & Company.

Edwards, B.(1986), *Drawing on the Artist Within*. London; Fontana Collins

Elgin, D, & Le Drew, C. (1997) *Global Consciousness Change: Indications of an Emerging Paradigm*. San Anselmo, CA

Frankel, V. (1963) *Man's Search for Meaning*. New York: Simon & Schuster

Fromm, Erich. (1957) *The Art of Loving*. London:Thorsons

Gray, J. (1992) *Men are from Mars Women are from Venus*; New York; Harper and Collins

Goethe, J W., (1962) *Faust* New York; Anchor

Gleick, J. (1999) *Faster*. London: Little Brown.

Golman, D. (1995) *Emotional Intelligence*. New York: Bantam Books

Grof, S. (1998) *The Cosmic Game*. Dublin; Gill & McMillan

Hendrix, H. (1993) *Getting the Love you Want*. London: Simon & Schuster

Hammerschlag, C. (1994) *The Theft of Spirit*. New York: Fireside

Hoyle, F. (1983) *The Intelligent Universe*. London: Michael Joseph.

Humphreys,T. (2004)*The Power of Negative Thinking*. Dublin; New Leaf

Jung, C. (1983) *Man and his Symbols*. London: Picador

Kuhn, T. (1970) *The Structure of Scientific Revolutions*. Chicago

Koestler, A. (1964) *Act of Creation*, New York, Macmillan

Laslo, E. (1972) *The Introduction to Systems Philosophy*. New York: Gordon & Breach

Langer, E. J. (2005) *On Becoming an Artist*. New York: Random House

Langer, E. J. (1989) *Mindfullness,* Addison Wesley Publishing Company

Mah, A.Y. (2000) *Watching the Tree*. London: HarperCollins

May, R. (1975) *The Courage to Create*. New York: W.W. Norton &Company.

Maslow, A. (1954) *Motivation and Personality* Harper, New York

Maslow, A. (1964) *Religions, Values and Experiences*. Columbus (OH): Ohio State University Press.

Mayer, B. (2000).*The Dynamics of Conflict Resolution*. Jossey- Bass Publishers

Miller, A.. (1990), *The Drama of Being a Child*. London Virago Press Limited

Morison,Erickson,Dychtwald (2006) *Workforce Crisis*, Harvard University Press

Myers, L. (1980) *Gifts Differing*. Palo Alto: Consulting Psychological Press

Nukav, G. (1990) *The Seat of the Soul*. London: Rider & Co

Redfield Jamison, K. (2005) *Exuberance* New York. Vintage Books Random House

Ridley, M. (2003) *Nature Via Nurture* New York, Harper and Collins

Rodgers, C. (1976) *On Becoming a Person*. London: Constable

Rodgers, C. (1959) *Towards a Theory of Creativity in Creativity and Its Cultivation*, H. H Anderson New York Harper and Row

Rumi, J. (1999) *Selected Poems* London, Penguin Books

Senge, P. M. (1990)*The Fifth Discipline*; The *Art and Practice of the Learning Organization* Currency Doublesday

Sheldrake, R. (1984) *A New Science of Life*, Paladin Books London.

Sheldrake, R. (1988) *The Presence of the Past. Morphic Resonance and the Habits of Nature*. London: Collins

Storr, A.(1985, 1977) *The Dynamics of Creation*, Hamondsworth; Pelican, New York Atheneum

Sperry,R. (1977) *"Bridging Science and Values: A Unifying View of Mind and Science"*. *American Psychologist,* April 1977

Sheehy, G. (1982) *Pathfinders*. New York Bantam Books
Sheldrake, R. (1988) *The Presence of the Past. Morphic Resonance and the Habits of Nature. London,* Collins
Storr, A. (1988)*Solitude; A Return to Self.* Ballantine,
Tice, Baumeister, (1993) "*Controlling Anger; Self Induced Emotion Change*" quoted in Wegner and Pennebaker eds. *Handbook of Mental Control.* Prentice Hall
Ury, Fisher, (1981) *Getting to Yes.* Boston: Houghton Mifflin.
Wells, S. (2005) *The Oxford Shakespeare.*2nd Ed, Oxford, Oxford Press
White, D. (1994) The *Heart Aroused* Currency Doubleday
Wheatley, M. J. (1994) *Leadership and the New Science; Learning about Organization from an orderly Universe.* Barrett-Koehler, Inc.
Wark, M. (2007) *Gamer Theory* Harvard University Press